# When A Glass Breaks

# When A Glass Breaks

Ed Renner

Copyright © 2010 by Ed Renner.

| Library of Congress Control Number: | | 2010901465 |
| ISBN: | Hardcover | 978-1-4500-3761-7 |
| | Softcover | 978-1-4500-3760-0 |
| | Ebook | 978-1-4500-3762-4 |

All rights reserved. No part of this book may be reproduced or transmitted in any form or by any means, electronic or mechanical, including photocopying, recording, or by any information storage and retrieval system, without permission in writing from the copyright owner.

This book was printed in the United States of America.

**To order additional copies of this book, contact:**
Xlibris Corporation
1-888-795-4274
www.Xlibris.com
Orders@Xlibris.com
74718

*CIRCA 2002*
*AND BEFORE . . . . AND BEYOND*

# INTRODUCTION

HALF EMPTY OR half full. It's a metaphor for attitude. The optimist sees the glass as half full. The pessimist . . . . half empty. One revels in the prospect of filling the glass all the way to the top. The other contemplates, drip by drip, that soon there will be emptiness. Like emptiness in his sorry life.

When a glass breaks, the symbolism is profound. If the glass is destroyed, then there will be thousands—perhaps, of sharp, destructive chards, ready to cut and injure. If the glass is symbolic of a society, then the society, which used to be smooth and intact, now has to contend with sharp, cunning "dissidents". The liquid inside the glass spreads and becomes part of something else, no longer having its identity. If the liquid were instead, a metaphor for people, then they would lose their very being, disappearing into a much bigger mass. They are, for all intents and purposes, gone. At the very least, changed forever.

This is a story about a series of events that shatter that which was once tranquil. In this story, when the "glass breaks", life changed instantly.

Lives were lost. Lives were irreparably damaged.

The effects of a tragedy . . . . it is about Gene Shanahan, an ordinary, yet angry man and his wife, Geri. It's a trip back into his life and yet a current story. It's about a still unanswered question.

Is there really an afterlife? Gene faces this mystery first hand when Geri, at one point, professes her undying love for him. "If I die first, you'd better find me in Heaven". What if she wasn't there?

# ONE

EVERYWHERE THEY WENT, he would drive. And, unlike a lot of guys, when Saturday and Sunday came, all Gene wanted was to be with her. Geri was the nicest person he had ever been around. Gene and Geri Shanahan. The flavors of every month.

They'd worked together for a couple of years. Gene would watch her at the office. Nothing ever rattled her. The boss was just plain evil. And Geri worked directly for him. She was beautiful. He was obnoxious. So she had two jobs. One was to be his right hand. The second was to keep track of his left. One day, she would escape to another job. Ruby's loss was Gene's gain.

He would sit at his desk sometimes and just wait until she passed by. The glass wall made it easy for him to have full view. When she walked, it was an event. Now, they were together. And they fit. Both had been the wrong half of other relationships. Now, they were the other's salvation.

So, there was no golf for him, no fishing, no card game. He wasn't looking for an excuse to get out of the house.

Shopping was not shopping. It was entertainment for him. He would drive the cart. He always drove. She would stop at all 10,000 products at the local warehouse club. This amazed Gene. Guys go shopping—stop, look, buy . . . gone. Not with Geri. Every step forward became two steps backward as she saw something else to go back to. Stop. Go. Stop. Go. His back hated her.

And he could never quite get the "back box" thing. If they wanted cereal, she would move all the boxes in front until she could reach no farther back. Then she would take that one. "What's wrong with these?" he would ask.

Never got an answer. So, he would drive the cart. She would drive him crazy. But, to him, it beat the best golf course in the state.

Gene was a pragmatic sort. For this reason, he never got too overwhelmed with anything. He would just reason his way through whatever was placed in front of him. Sooner or later, a conclusion or resolution would show itself. For this reason, he was very good at his job.

He hated the "computer generation". They have lost the ability to reason, he would say. Two and two is five, that famous joke, was now aptly passed on to computer geeks.

Geri was altogether different. If a story had ten pages, she would start at Page 5. There were many conversations, where Gene hadn't had a clue what she was talking about. This would make him laugh some times and see red at other times. Mostly, it was cute.

# TWO

THE WEATHER GUY on TV has a bag over his head. He screwed up the forecast. Mea Culpa. The anchor people begin and end each story by giving the county where it happened. This drives Gene crazy. Worse yet, it seems like every county in the state has a Turkey Hill that was robbed last night. Turkey Hills grow up to be 7/11's, he thought. Gene wonders how this can keep happening. Small time towns. Or, is it counties. Small time cops, Gene thought.

He and Geri had a regimen. Every morning at 5:00AM, they had their coffee and their twenty minutes in bed watching the local yokul news. Gene would lose patience and commandeer the "clicker". Switch to the New York stations where there was real crime. But, inevitably, he would switch back. This is something he couldn't explain. There wasn't a beauty to be seen on the local news. This was network purgatory. Local affiliate. Local yokuls. The sports guy opened his segment with High School football. High School basketball. High School this and High School that. Gene, a kid from New York, thought he died and went to Mayberry. "Show me the Mets, for Christ sake". When they did get to the big leagues, it was the Philly teams! The king of the clicker went back and forth, from New York to Hooterville, in Hooterville County, of course. Gene found that the more he clicked, the more he settled on Hooterville. Strange. It was getting to him. But, looking at the bright side, there was more ammunition for him to work his humor with the yokuls. He was a very funny man. Geri had a front row seat every morning for Gene's comedic tirade. Something for everyone, he was an "equal opportunity" critic.

He was working on writing a book. Everybody has said this at one time or another. It's a loose promise, like a politician's pledge. He even had a title, "Who Asked?" Who, indeed. It would be less of a story, but more a list of angry conclusions that he had reached over all his years. He was always a bit angry.

So, every morning was the same. Wake up, sit up, watch 20 minutes of the news, think and ponder. His mind moved faster than the anchor's teleprompter. God knows there was enough in there. Years of abnormalcy.

Geri had done a beautiful job of arranging pictures on the hall wall. There were five generations of "forget me nots" on the wall. It was amazing, really, that so much time has gone by and that someone cared enough, as Geri did, to construct this eight by ten foot museum. From his vantage point, Gene could see his son Chris's picture. He was in full football uniform. He had a twenty two hundred dollar smile in his mouth and a million dollar smile in his eyes. Now the picture was all that he had.

It had been three years since Chris drove into a tree and was lost. As the story goes, he was reaching for his cell phone. Took his eyes off the road for a split second and never felt the car moving across the solid line. It was a head on collision.

Chris never wore his seatbelt. "I'm gonna live forever", he would say. In a way, Gene rationalized that Chris would be twenty years old and Harry Connick—handsome forever.

Gene could bear no more than a "one evening" wake. His wife was catatonic. His daughter didn't even attend. She said that she wanted to remember her hunky brother as a vibrant, very much alive female magnet. Gene couldn't argue with this.

He and his wife had to be there. At one point, one of Chris' friends hung over a slumped Mr. and Mrs. Shanahan, like a gray cloud that wouldn't move. Gene looked up to receive the obligatory condolence. It was the first outward response from Gene. "I lost my boy". The kid looked down at Gene, never missed a moment, responded immediately—"You didn't lose your boy, Mr. Shanahan. He's just not here anymore". For the rest of his life, Gene would take comfort in this two sentence antiseptic. But, for the rest of his life, Gene would nurture bitterness. It was always there, just below his smile.

# THREE

AS WITH MOST families, times have not been easy for Gene's. Close families, he concluded, were really called that because they were hiding secrets, hiding imperfections. And they would close ranks in a sometimes vain attempt to fight off all the problems that life had to offer. When you go to war with somebody, you become closer to your comrade in arms. It's the survival of battle that makes people close. This was Gene's assessment of what a close family really is. His first marriage, which had produced his Army, his son and daughter, was a lost battle.

From the time of Chris' funeral, Cassidy, Gene's daughter, changed. She was loving. She was beautiful. She was smart. But she became distant. Perhaps she was just exercising the rites of adolescence. The result was painful nonetheless. And Gene blamed every negative change in his life on Chris' passing.

But, all these years later, he had his two contributions to add to Geri's wall. Geri was the mother to the prettiest little girl in the world, Jeannie. They were as close as close is. Gene could count on one visit a year from Cassie, if that. The phone calls were non-existent. Although he shouldn't have, he took what he could get. But, there was resentment. Along with Geri's daughter, their two past unions produced enough people for him to think that there was a shot at one of them succeeding in life. It was a hope, anyway. With Chris now gone . . . . or, not here, it was up to Cassie and Jeannie.

The two were quite different. Jeannie was sensitive and genuinely loving. This, Gene concluded, was because Geri, herself, was loving. This axiom, somehow, didn't manifest itself with Cassie. Why? He would ask. He was a good person. But, he was also the one who moved out of the house and left his marriage. He moved. Inconvenienced a lot of lives. Starting with his. He has paid ever since.

Last night, while Gene watched a movie, the main character quoted John F. Kennedy. "An error becomes a mistake if it doesn't get corrected." This struck Gene hard, like a 16 pound bowling ball hitting a two pound pin. Over the years, he worked hard, very hard, at building a successful father / child relationship. He wouldn't say that he was trying to correct an error. His children were no error. Gene loved them very much. And correction was the wrong word. But he saw some similarity in JFK's words.

So far, Cassie carried herself like the lazy student who didn't do her homework, the one who didn't learn that lesson, the one who was absent that day. Gene wasn't a quitter. He tries and he tries and he tries again. Once, while in therapy, his doctor, who had had his own challenges with his son, told him that the boy didn't "come around" until he was 30 years old. Stop the presses, there was still hope.

So, he's sitting in his usual position in bed, watching the TV with one eye and staring at all those pictures with the other.

# FOUR

"SIT UP STRAIGHT, young man!" Sister Mary Godzilla, taking all of her sexual frustrations out on her class of urchins. Eight year old Eugene, nicknamed Eenie, at the time, tended to slouch as he did at home, ducking the next slap from his tough guy father. It would take 30 years before Eenie would understand the mindset of a bully. Cowards really.

St. Monica's was a small grammar school tucked in the middle of a lower west side neighborhood in the "city". It could be any city. But, in this case, it was New York. There weren't any children of privilege in this school. It seemed that every kid's dad worked for a trucking company. Red Star Lines, Mid Hudson Trucking, Smith's, etc.

World War II was over. It was almost like all the young guys were told to report to the shop stewards and the dispatchers of the local branch of the "Everyman" Trucking Company. After that came the next order. Ok, Private, now fall in for lesson two of post war life: choosing the Gin Mill. There wasn't any mill at these places. Most of them didn't even drink gin! But, that's what they called it. It was a place where they could go after work to refill on courage. There, everyone hit .450.

There, everyone was Joe Lewis and Jack Dempsey.

There, they were anyone they wanted to be, except themselves. Six beers and they were ready to go home and practice their abuse. Throw their wives a smack . . . because they needed it.

Home was a haven. A place where nobody fought back. Eugene's dad was a big man. He had a natural glare. So, he was avoided. Dad was selective. He only picked on smaller guys, kids and his wife. By day, at work, he was probably challenged by some of the other graduates of the University of Gin Mill. Somehow, however, by the time that he got home, during that 30 minute walk, he would conjure up the swashbuckling heroics of his day.

By about the sixth beer, dad was ready to fight. He saw his son as the natural punching bag. Shorter by seven inches, lighter by 70 lbs. About right for Dad. Home Sweet Home.

# FIVE

"**M**ORE COFFEE SWEETHEART?" Gene was back. It's amazing, he thought, how much memory a person can conjure up in just a minute or so. It's even more amazing that these images of his dad were right there on the wall in the hall. Gene even wore his dad's 25 year Teamster retirement watch, as an honor to the departed terrorist.

Go figure, he would say to himself. Geri brought two more cups back to bed, while they finished watching the news. "Are you OK?" she asked. Of course. "Why wouldn't I be?" he challenged, always ready for battle.

Back to normal. The weather guy was doing the weather. The sports guy did the morning report. Bishop this beat Bishop that. Then came the community service bulletins. Things to do. Spaghetti Dinner down at Fire Department. *The Fire Department? Gene thought.* Bingo at the Town Hall. The Town Hall, for chrissake. Those only exist in cowboy movies, he thought.

This kid from Manhattan was woefully lost, drowning in Americana. "Is this really normal, he thought?"

5:22AM. Ok, time to move. Right on schedule. Fully prepared for the day. As he got out of bed, now in full view of the pictures, he wondered who was crazy, the hay shakers on TV or him. They, at least, looked happy. All's right with the world. Joe Jones' pig finally passed gas, the potholes on Stanton St. got paved and the Turkey Hill got robbed.

In just four steps down the hall, he was now eight years older. A High School picture befitting of the 10 most wanted down at the Post Office. He thought for a minute about the sports report he had just watched. When he was in High School, it wasn't like that. He always looked older than he was. So, sneaking into the bar for a beer was no problem. Instead of trying out for this team or that, Eugene had to get a job.

He didn't have to. He just didn't feel right, taking money from his parents. He was old enough to work. The shame of it was that he was a terrific, if unmolded, athlete. During his freshman year at Cardinal so and so High School, he was talked into running the mile race at Freshman Day. The events were held at Randall's Island Stadium in Manhattan. City blocks were small. Eugene had no idea how long a mile really was. 20 blocks, someone had told him. Didn't seem much. He dressed in his gym uniform and made his way to the field. There was this huge running track. He gasped. "How do I make it around that track?"

Once around, he thought. How bad could it be? Then they gave him the news . . . 4 times around! It was that day that he learned how to hold a complete conversation with himself. He was completely delusional, ready to pass out. But, as he completed the fourth lap, all he wanted now was to finish. And finish he did. First Place!

The following Monday, they gave out the medals. Gene finished first. But all they had left were bronze medals. He didn't know it at the time but there, on that day, he got a glimpse of what would be much of his life.

# SIX

FOURTEEN NOW. RUNNING! Johnny and Gene were fast. Very fast. As they're eating up track, Gene is wondering why, in the hell, they're running. "What happened, Gene asked?"

Johnny said that as they turned the corner, he caught a glimpse of the 12th Street Boys. How great was that, Eugene thought. They had a title, like in the movies. The James Gang. The Magnificent Seven. Johnny was one of the tough kids in the neighborhood. *So, why were they running?* After a while, they met two more of their friends, Kevin and YooHoo. YooHoo was named after the chocolate drink. We all wondered why. One day, he told us that his real name was Clarence Leon Randolph Zewitzky. *Hey, Gene thought, YooHoo! Works for me.*

So, there they were. Who was better than them? Well, the 12th St. gang thought they were. They came around the corner to the left. Circling around, like dogs looking for rear ends.

*There's a sight, he thought. What does a dog do anyway. Sniff a good ass and then . . . . "how ya doin, I'm Max." One of the mysteries of life.*

Nobody moved. This is what you did when you were either ready for the fight or the bathroom, whichever was appropriate at the time. They seemed to favor Gene. One of them unwrapped his faux courage and sent a swift kick between Gene's legs. Fortunately for Gene, the kick landed two inches beyond his jewels. Never felt it. His reputation was formed right then and there. His assailant couldn't believe it. He didn't have a follow. Unfortunately for Gene, one of the other 12th St. mutts did. He searched the nearby garbage cans for a weapon. Damned if he didn't find one. It was an old, discarded Porcelain Kitchen Clock. He threw it to the ground and it shattered into six or seven usable "knives". 12th St. picked one up and sliced at Gene. Christ, all they needed was Leonard Bernstein. And where was Officer Krupke when you needed him. Gene raised his left arm to shield him from a blow.

The clock struck. Gene's elbow was bleeding. But he didn't go down. 12th St. turned to look at his friends.

They looked like confused puppies. 12th St. jumped at Gene. In one motion, 12th St. was down. Now, one of the others stepped forward. Gene sent him to the ground. None of Gene's friends did anything. It was one against four.

They all fell before the new bull in town. It was over as fast as it began. It dawned on Gene that his tough buddies were nowhere to be found in this, the Battle of Abingdon Square.

But, there they were, strutting down the street. They had defeated the dreaded 12thStreeters.

Crossing Hudson St., they came upon three more of their friends. Gene's buddy, Kevin, ran ahead of them. His enthusiasm got the best of him before he even reached the other guys. "Genie just kicked the 12th Streeter's asses!"

Joy in Mudville! The jubilance was obvious, but the guys never moved. Strange. Out from behind them came Genie's father. "Oh God", Gene thought. "It's over". Instead, the King of the Block looked at his son and couldn't contain his joy. Now, Gene was a fighter too.

# SEVEN

THE BEDROOM WAS stylish. Gerri had a touch for accessories. Candles enhanced their romance. Lot's of statues. Lots of animals. There was a 6 foot tall giraffe in the corner, a turtle on the floor and a rocking horse next to the dresser. Somehow, it all went together.

On top of the dresser was something Gene never understood. It was a Barbie Doll. The kind with the beautiful face and the little clothes that would capture hours of a little girl's time. Comb the hair, change the outfits. Have the tea parties . . .

But, this Barbie was different. One of her arms was missing and one of her feet was broken off at the toes. Whenever Gene would ask her to throw the thing in the garbage, Gerri got angry and told him to mind his own business. She wasn't going to discard little Barbie. "Next subject" she would say.

Gene dropped it.

# EIGHT

GENE WAS SAVORING his last few minutes in bed. He had ten more minutes before he started the job of making the now 50 year old body look "12th Street tough". Damn, these pictures took him back. As he thought about his rumble—*"boy, boy, crazy boy, play it cool, boy*—he realized the things he learned that day. Tough is just a veneer. The wood under the surface is sometimes pine, not oak. The other thing he learned is that sometimes it's better to be lucky. Tell that to the 1990 Giants, who became Super Bowl heroes merely because the other team's kicker couldn't find one extra foot of accuracy, Gene thought. People remember what they want to remember. It's easier that way.

(excerpts from "Who Asked") If Adam and Eve were the only two people on the earth, then we are all a product of incest.

In today's sports world, when you score a goal or hit a home run or make a basket, you're supposed to look like you want to kill somebody.

Why do politicians never answer a question with a direct answer and then wonder why fewer and fewer people vote.

I never understood the expression, "the Babe Ruths of the world", the Frank Sinatras of the world. I imagine that there might be one or two more Frank Sinatras in the world, but the speaker, using this expression, probably doesn't even know the guy.

How come today's team athlete does something good, like score a touchdown or sink the game winning basket, and the first thing he does is separate himself from his teammates and raises his hands to the crowd, looking for applause. Team sports have suffered greatly. The coach, AKA the boss, makes less money than the ingrates that are called today's players. So, how does he get the players to listen.

Earrings and ponytails on men. What's next? Poodle skirts?????

# NINE

JUST BEFORE GENE unfolds his body from bed, the Hair Club commercial comes on. Goddamn commercials are so loud, he thought. This one was particularly distasteful. Gene's hair was getting thinner than floss. He always knew he would have to do something sooner or later. Boy, there's a story he's told before . . . . Twenty now. Out for a night of beer and women and music. They did Man 101 in Rockaway Beach, NY. To them, it was the country. An Irish neighborhood, it had a bar on every corner. Patty's Pub, The Blarney Stone, McGuinn's. Always a good band going. Gene was a voracious music fan. He grew up on DooWop and then the bands. First came The Beatles and all the other mop tops from England. American music changed as well. The vocal groups were replaced by bands.

It was both good and bad. The Young Rascals replaced The Cleftones. But, since the change was just beginning, all the bar bands played both. It was a fun time to be young.

On this particular night, one of the guys invited a friend from school. An Italian kid, named Tony (Sal, Vito?). He lived in the section of the city called little Italy. It was interesting that all these Italians ended up in one place. If they wanted to stay with Italians, why'd they move from Italy in the first place? Plenty of Italians to live with right there in Big Italy, Gene thought.

It was the usual night for the boys. Johnny just sat and drank as much beer as he could consume. Yoo Hoo and Gene were God's gift to any deserving woman. And Ken was just happy to laugh with his college buddies. It was way out in Rockaway, but everyone converged there. The usual ending. Nobody scored. Johnny was legless and Ken was cold sober.

Three in the morning. The boys were almost home. First, they had to drop Mario (?) off. The car belonged to Ken. He drove. Kenny was a nice sort, but kind of matronly, in a boy's kind of way. He brought the car to a halt, on Mulberry St., just inside of Mott St. Buena Sera, Vincenzo. The boy with ten names went into his building. Ken and the boys headed back to the car. At that very moment, another car rounded the corner, couldn't stop in time and introduced itself to the bumper of Ken's very uncool Plymouth Valiant.

In the other car, just one guy, with his girlfriend. Ken did what anyone would do at 3:00AM in someone else's neighborhood. He asked the other guy for his license and insurance information.

The other driver, probably operating with a full tank of Johnny Walker Black, refused. "Fuck you, I ain't givvin yiz nuttin'"! He was nice and loud in the 3:00 AM air. The sound resonated like a helicopter, taking off in a Church. Maybe, he wasn't so drunk after all. Ken was getting nowhere with his diplomacy.

It was only a year ago that Ken was preparing for the seminary. Before the world got to him. The world was giving him a lesson now. Gene stepped forward, trying to use a tact more appropriate to the street. The "fucks" were flying. Two minutes later, another car conveniently snuck behind the Gigolo's car. It was a one way street.

Two more cars joined them, but coming up the one way street, the wrong way. Or the right, if you were them. Six in each car. And they weren't boys. And they weren't there for Bingo. Eighteen against four. "Oh shit" is the last thing Genie remembered saying.

Hit whoever you don't recognize and run, he thought. The Sons of The Old country were winning. It wasn't enough that they had the numbers in their favor. They had knives and even a hammer. Before Gene was introduced to the hammer, he remembered looking up at the tenements. The windows were dotted with spectators! Now, he was sitting on the street, leaning against a car. Sitting there, asking the ridiculous question . . . . "What are you doing?" At that point, the "judge" brought down the hammer. Gene was still sitting. The hammer found its mark on Gene's head. Then he was out.

# TEN

NOW, ON A July morning almost thirty-three years later, Gene was sitting up on the bed almost ready to start his day. The last thing on TV was the "sell" line in the commercial—"Remember, I'm not just the President, I'm also a client." Gene, with the 120 stitches clearly visible under his angel hair, thought to himself, "I have to do something very soon." Then, the last thing on his mind, before he left the bed, was another flashback. His father visited him in the hospital once during the two weeks that it would take to insert a plate in his skull. To him, Gene had run from this fight. Dad never forgave him for that.

# ELEVEN

GENE RAN THE National Sales Division of a small company. His office was in New Jersey. Yet he lived in Pennsylvania. He wasn't the luckiest guy around when it came to his job proximity. When he lived in New York, he worked in New Jersey.

It's been 200 plus miles of driving daily as far back as he can remember. Now, in his "fifties", he resigned himself to the fact that all things considered, he was pretty lucky.

The owner of the company was a despicable human being. There were no bounds to the unprofessionalism that this man exhibited.

The company was on a roll. Gene was no small part of this. Yet, the owner, Sol Rubenstein, somehow didn't have enough to pay his vendors. Gene's view was that he was the owner, the guy who took all the risks. And so it was his right to run the company in any way he saw fit. It's a free country. If it bothered any of Sol's minions, they were always free to leave. Because of his excellent income, Gene would stay.

Some of the antics really bothered him. Sol–Ruby, as he became known, set up a fake Travel Agency. All of the traveling staff had stickers that they were to place on legitimate airline tickets. This would result in lower fares. Nobody liked this part of it. But, everybody did it. They all needed their jobs.

The worst offense that Gene saw had to do with the packaging of defective returned products and reshipping them. So, as long as the company received Returned Defective Merchandise, Ruby was never out of stock during those times when the factories weren't being paid and, therefore, refused to release orders. It was truly a dangerous, albeit illegal, game. But, it was self fulfilling. Make junk, it comes back, often; repackage it and send it out again. Boomerangs.

It was always a complete mystery that the company did any business. Gene had, in another life, built successful divisions for legitimate companies. His specialty was the auto radio aftermarket business. The business, during

Gene's tenure, had grown to be quite sophisticated. The new equipment made the inside of a car sound like a concert hall. Yet, Ruby's company was selling $30.00 car radios that didn't even rewind a tape. The world was buying CD's, but Ruby was making his fortune selling, and reselling, this junk to the Mass Merchants. Gene figured that he must have pictures of the key buyers doing sex acts with cows. Otherwise how, when there were bigger companies out there, could Ruby hold onto these customers. But, the experience of it all gave Gene a new perspective on the American marketplace. Seeing all this "junk" get bought and sold, he called upon one of his father's favorite expressions . . . . "There's an ass for every seat".

Gene's immediate boss was a story in itself. One day Ruby called Gene into his office. Ruby told him that they would be visited by a gentleman at two o'clock. If Gene liked him, the guy would come aboard to work for Gene. 2:00PM rolled around and the gentleman arrived. Gene saw him through the glass wall of his office. But he was on the phone and couldn't greet the visitor for a few minutes.

Holding a conversation on the phone and staring at the visitor, Gene couldn't help noticing the absolute look of despair on his face. The phone conversation was finished, the introduction was made and Gene went about the tour of the company with his new charge. When they were finished, Gene took the man to Ruby's office, wished him well and went back to his office. One hour later, Gene was called into Ruby's office and introduced to his new boss. Emerging from the short meeting, Gene was white. "What just happened in there?" It was, thank God, Friday afternoon. There was no more concentration on work. All he could think about was Gerri.

The living room of their home was elegant. Gerri had an amazing talent for decorating. Marble tables, candles, music. And tonight, wine, lots of wine. Cabernet Sympathy, 2001. "Bottle of red, bottle of white, in the kind of mood you're in tonight." (Gene's idol, Billy Joel).

# TWELVE

HELLO! HELLO! I say, old man, hello! It was the best impression of a British butler that Gene had heard in years. It was Sebastian Cabot, Terry Thomas and John Cleese, all rolled into one. Throw in The Nanny's butler for good measure. And it came out of the mouth of this self-appointed success story from Brooklyn. Isaac was Gene's new boss. The man fancied himself as cultured. Yet, in a restaurant, when Isaac didn't feel bathed in enough admiration and attention, he would break out his best, most condescending tones for the wait staff.

The guy never quite grasped that he was bringing attention to himself, all right. This brought about another talent. Only this talent belonged to the waiters and waitresses. They could actually smile and mumble asshole, under their breath, for all the world to see, except Isaac. Smart as a whip and dumber than shit, at the same time.

The true meaning of the word Arrogant. This was Isaac. Apparently, he didn't taste the ashes in his soup that the smiling minion placed it in front of him.

Like most bullies, Isaac's act was just a shell of insecurity. An uncooked egg. Hard shell outside, slime inside. Underneath this Cary Grant was a decent guy. But, a boy really had to look for it. From the beginning, Gene let Isaac know that he wasn't the least bit intimidated. Hell, Gene was a veteran of ten rounds a night with his father, another bully. So they had an understanding. Check your act at the door and there wouldn't be a problem. Isaac knew nothing of the business that he was now running. Gene was the expert that he needed.

Gene hated every conversation with Ruby. Isaac intimidated the hell out of the boss. As long as there was an Isaac, there would be peace with Ruby. In a way, Isaac was a Godsend. Peaceful, resentful coexistence.

~30~

"I can promise you one thing", Isaac said to Gene. "We'll have fun". Damned if he wasn't right. Isaac loved sports. Gene loved sports. Plenty to talk about.

And they both grew up listening to Doo Wop music. Gene loved his Doo Wop music. There was, he thought, enough common ground to make this work. Whenever they would discuss a particular guy, a buyer that they had just called on or a sales rep, Gene immediately placed him out front of his very own virtual singing group. Ruby and The Romantics was an easy one. But there was Al and the Fabulous Cadillacs, Craig and the On-the-Take Tones, and so on. It wasn't so bad, Gene thought. The Yankees were Isaac's team. Gene was a Met fan. It was just a year ago that New York was in a frenzy, watching their two teams play each other in the World Series. An actual Subway series. Of course, the Yankees won. But Gene's Mets were there. It was a great week or so.

Lately Gene found himself thinking of the past. A lot of memories were relived. Gene wondered why all of these old memories were bouncing around his brain lately. His most logical conclusion was that, in times of stress in life, people might tend to revisit the past. Especially those times that were good. Those parts of his life were gone. They couldn't be changed. In a way, when people conjure up the old times, they are completely eliminating the possibility of surprise. They become in full control, something that he could use right now.

So, it came as no surprise that when Gene and Isaac began to discuss their respective teams, memories of long ago visited Gene. When he was nineteen, Gene had a tryout, at Shea Stadium, with The New York Mets! He always had guts. A friend of his talked him into writing to the team for a tryout. The funny part was that Gene had never played a game of baseball in his life. In Manhattan, there were no baseball fields. Everybody played softball. He was a very good softball player. "Hey, how different can it be", he asked. Never did he think that he would actually be invited by The Mets. But, the letter came. Gene had to borrow a baseball uniform. Three sizes too small. He looked like Little Abner or The Incredible Hulk. It would be fun, he thought. There would be nothing incredible about his performance unless, of course, you were The Mets. He and his friend would have a great time.

When the day came, Gene's friend was nowhere to be found. So, he hopped the subway and went by himself. Getting dressed in the Visitor's locker room was an amazing thrill. Playing catch alongside the dugout was awesome. From there, it was awful. First, everyone had to race. Pretty smart, thought Gene. The first cut would be guys who were slow. He, on the other hand, was lightning. Groups of threes, running from home plate, down the line, all the way to the right field warning track. The Hulk won his race. "What's your name, son?" A big kid who could run.

All down hill from there. All of the outfielders were directed to Center Field. *"Put me in coach, I'm ready to play today"*. Each player had to field five balls, some flies, some line drives and grounders.

No particular order. They had to catch the balls, throw twice to second base, twice to third base, once to the plate. Then they were done. They were called in alphabetical order. Gene was thrilled to be a Shanahan. It was the most family pride he had shown in decades. Actually, it was first time he thought about his heritage.

As the balls were heading for the "A" players, and the "H" players, he studied the trajectory of each ball. "Go back, go back, go in, go in". To his surprise, Gene got it right most of the time. Judgement, he knew, would be different than a softball.

"Shanahan! Ok son, let's see what you can do". Gene felt for sure that they had offered him this warm greeting because he did so well in the run trials. First ball. It stayed up there forever. But he had a good beat on it. The problem was that it never came down. Landed forty feet behind him. *"Oh shit!"* After that a ground ball. Gene scooped it up and delivered a crisp 75 bounce throw that barely reached the second baseman.

The rest was just as painful. But he had made the first list of names called . . . the cut list. The 19 year old softball phenom wasn't devastated. Quite the opposite, it would become, literally, one of the treasured events of his lifetime.

Now the "fifty something" ex-softball phenom looks at the experience a little differently. Two ways, actually. One was tremendous pride in the courage that it took to show up. Two was much more pragmatic—"I must have been fuckin' crazy". To this day, the Letter of Invitation from The New York Metropolitan Baseball Club hangs proudly in a five dollar frame. It was something like framing your draft notice, he thought. Very official, but it was nothing more than an invitation to a dance full of ugly girls. Gene never told the "tryout" story to Isaac. They weren't really close. Besides, the arrogant prick would probably come up with something to top it.

# THIRTEEN

WHEN RUBY VISITED his major accounts, he went in force. Himself, Isaac, Gene, and Ruby's son. The son, Seth, was a pleasant enough kid who was obviously along to carry all the samples. *"Oh what a circus, Oh what a show . . ."*

There were many trips like this. Run to the airport, run to a meeting, do the presentation and run back to the airport. On one trip, Isaac and Gene got separated from Ruby and Norman. Ruby was wearing a full length, oversized green top coat, and a very wide brimmed hat, like a fedora from Capone's vault. Gene took in the folly of it all, leaned over to Isaac's ear and broke into song, borrowed from the old Batman TV Series . . . "na na na na na na na na na na na na na na na na hatman!". Isaac was laughing so hard that he almost didn't make the Men's Room.

# FOURTEEN

THE DRIVE TO the office was more like a pilgrimage. Gene lived his life, he thought, with a car seat stuck to his ass. Coming out of his lakeside community, he was on his way. About three miles, down the small country highway, was a brand new Pizza Shop. When it first opened, Gene thought, Wow, how good was that! Owning a business just around the corner from your house.

There was a new high school just down the street. There was a new Police Department next to the high school. He thought, for sure, that the owner would make a killing. But the place never had cars there. Gene could imagine the owner putting his life savings into this "can't miss" business.

He felt sorry for the guy. Just a matter of time before it closed. It was for this reason that Gene had never tried something like that himself. At least he had a job. A very demanding job, but a job nonetheless. A job he hated and had to drive for hours to get to. But, a job.

As he walked into the office, he was immediately taken by the sullenness of all the faces. This was a place that nobody liked going to. Isaac was in his office. He saw Gene. Called him into his office. Gene knew what was coming. Isaac would make notes the night before. Twenty new questions for Gene, each representing a day's work in itself. "I'm still working on the twenty from two days ago!" After a while, Gene figured out that, if he just listened to Isaac's ranting and then go about his day, Isaac would forget half the things that were so important. And, tomorrow, there'd be twenty more projects. My God, Gene thought, how in the hell did I ever end of in this position. *"We gotta get out of this place, if it's the last thing we ever do"*, Gene and the Fabulous Frustrations.

Every day Ruby would have his meeting. Same as Isaac's. What are we doing here? What are we doing there? No discussion of the last plane trip and circus. Ruby was just happy to go from place to place, make his presentations with his entourage and go on to the next one.

The buyers at these dog and pony shows were shell shocked. Look at this. What do you think of that. Here are four more products that we put together just for you. Interesting that they were the same products that were put together just for last week's caravan.

Nothing ever came of these presentations. Gene could sense that the buyers just couldn't wait to get everybody the hell out of his office. Gene worked in an entirely different way. There was a purpose to his sales presentations. This is what we have. This is how it compares to your present product mix. These are our advantages.

This is why you should buy ours. Simple. Digestable. Successful. But the Ruby and Isaac National Tour was, they would say, the way to do it in this business. Pay attention to us, son. You'll learn. Gene had created Divisions for other companies that did more business than Ruby's entire company. How he hated working for these clowns.

On most mornings, Gene would stop at St. Ann's before heading to the office. They had a 6:00AM Mass. Nobody ever there. Gene thought it some kind of punishment for the priests who had to say Mass. God must be punishing them for something.

It was quiet. Although there was a Mass going on, Gene never stayed. He would just clutch the church pew like a dying man clings to a rosary. Dying's funny. When you know it's your time, if you're lucky, you begin to do one of two things . . . . make things right with your maker or go through the motions, hoping that the man above isn't paying attention long enough for you to slip past the gates.

So there was Gene, dying emotionally, wanting to make things right. When he was divorced, he endured much the same as he had his whole life. His daughter wanted nothing to do with him. His childhood was challenging, his marriage a failure, his job a train wreck. He needed help so, he turned to St. Ann's and to the Man. He would sit and talk. Not aloud, but under his breath. He would thank the Man for giving him Geri. He would ask that his daughter be taken care of, and he would say various prayers for various people in need at the time. Gene had spent so many years denying God's existence. It was a combination of pragmatism and self pity. Now he valued his visits. It made him feel that he had some worth. Through all the stages of his life, he would gravitate back to the church, any church, and he would stare in disbelief into nowhere in particular.

WHEN A GLASS BREAKS

He was trying to make some sense of all the incredible bad luck that he had. *"Some folks' lives roll easy, some folks' lives never roll at all"*. Gene thought Paul Simon a prophet for having written that one.

The bank of candles that every church has now cost an incredible $3.00 each to light. Gene, the Sales Manager, thought that to be the best bit of sales he ever saw. He always felt that his life would finally be resolved when the entire first row was burning brightly, each flame reaching with its hot hand toward the heavens. Or, was it the ceiling?

# FIFTEEN

IT WAS A Monday morning. Gene rolled up to work, on time. Isaac was already in his office. Isaac was always on fire on Mondays. All the sale circulars were in Sunday's paper. Whoever was promoting whatever, was in the circulars. Isaac would read the circulars like a good novel. No doubt he was good at his profession. Then the 100 questions. "Why aren't we here? Do we have any ads coming up?" For all of his talent, Gene didn't quite grasp the fact that these circulars drove the entire business. There was EVERYDAY and there was ON AD. Normally, Gene loved learning stuff like this. New things to learn about selling. This was as exciting to him as a jug of cheap wine was to a derelict. But, all Gene ever felt was attacked. *Jesus, can I get my coat off, he thought.*

The morning went by as normal. Gene would talk to his sales team. They were all from different businesses. None really knew much about selling to the Mass Merchant trade. Only Isaac. The funny part was that all three guys were hand picked by Isaac and forced on Gene. The guy had to be dominant. Why would he hire guys who had no immediate entrees into the big accounts? Isaac, the hero, the expert. Inferiority complex 101.

Lunch at the diner was always the same. Isaac always had a tuna fish salad on toast. He had a scruffy beard, strange for a guy who considered himself so sartorial. The tuna fish salad always found its way to his beard. Gene had to make conversation, all the while staring at this buffoon's face, which resembled the dish that the sandwich came on.

# SIXTEEN

ROSIE'S PLACE. THAT'S what everybody in the office called it. Ruby had installed a cafeteria for the employees, referred to by him as Associates, as if they were his equals. In reality, it was an assurance that Ruby would have his peons under his nose for the entire day. No one should go outside for lunch. Lunch was here. Rosie ran this private restaurant. She was a sweet lady of Ecuadorian descent. She worked here. Her family was still in Ecuador. "No work in Ecuador, Angel", she would say. Everyone was "Angel". It sounded a little different in Spanglish, but it was still Angel.

Gene liked Rosie. He had tremendous respect for her. She was without her family too. Just like him. But his daughter was only a car ride away.

Her kids were in another world. She worked incessantly, trying to send as much money as possible to Ecuador. Someday, there would be enough to bring her family here, to the promised land. Somehow, Rosie was always cheerful. Genuinely glad to be there in Ruby's Greasy Spoon. Rosie's Place. "What I can make for jou, Angel?" Rosie and The Originals, Gene thought. "Angel Baby". *"It's just like heaven, being here with you"*. Rosie actually made everybody believe it.

Rosie's Place was a convenient getaway for the misery that was going on downstairs. Isaac and Gene were there constantly, having their meetings or just plain escaping Ruby's wrath.

# SEVENTEEN

THE BEST REMEDY for Gene, if he was going to survive working for this fruitcake, was to get lost in the field. He was a great salesman. He never went to an account without a purpose and a plan. So, it wasn't as if Gene was just traveling for the sake of traveling. There were always accounts to see, goods to sell and promotional ideas to be presented. He was constantly amazed that the bigger the customer, the easier it was to succeed. Everyone was so overworked that the goal of the job was lost as long as the paper was moving.

An expensive lunch or dinner was worth, at least, a sales promotion or two. Gene was engaging. He was sincere. Oftentimes, the buyer would bring his wife along for the "business" meal. Simple reason. These trysts were usually at the finest restaurants in town. Wines, at $100.00 per bottle, were the norm. Most of the wives loved Gene. He would always spend more time talking with the wives about their homes, their children, the dress they had on, the new hairstyle. He did this for no particular reason, other than the fact that he liked the women, most times, and wanted them to feel that they weren't brought there for the purpose of "window" dressing. Of course, there was a benefit. The buyer and the wife, having been entertained royally, went home happy. A happy buyer is a buyer with a pen in his hand the next day at the office.

# EIGHTEEN

B UTCH SULLIVAN WAS a train wreck. In his 47 years of existence on this earth, he hadn't done much but complain about his abusive father, his cowering mother and his inevitable path to destruction. Everyone was to blame except him. Strangely, or not, Butchie became the very person he bitched mostly about . . . his father. So many wasted years. Six years ago, something glorious happened in Butchie the Bozo's life. Her name was Nichole. And, as if the man upstairs was making up for lost time, along came this magnificent little angel into their lives. 1980 became the defining year of his pathetic life.

Butchie, the loser, was a father. Everything changed. Nikki and Butch named her Grace. They weren't sure why. A religious reference, as if an apology for the first part of his life? Or possibly a tribute to the first lady besides his mom that he ever noticed, Gracie Allen. She was the consummate comedic half of the George Burns and Gracie act. When he was a kid, Gracie made him laugh. Or could they have named little Gracie after the wild, walking protest that Butchie sang to, during his druggie days . . . . Gracie Slick. It could have been any or all three.

But this little Gracie turned his life around. Butch and Nichole followed the American dream a bit further. They adopted a dog. Gracie needed a playmate. A dog represented to Butchie the final piece to the American family. He never had a dog when he was a punching bag for his dad. The dog was named, of course, George. George and Gracie . . . perfect. George was a sorry looking mutt. A "Heinz 57", as they used to say so many years ago. 57 varieties. They could have gone to the pet store for a normal Gigi or Max. Instead, Butchie felt the need to rescue an abused, helpless mutt from the local pound.

George and Gracie became instant friends. He would follow her around the house. It was either protection or George knew that half of what Gracie was eating at the time, was his. The entire cookie never made it to her mouth. Half went to the floor. The floor belonged to George.

Butchie never had heroes from TV when he was four years old. But, how things have changed. Gracie would sit in front of the TV and talk to Bert, Ernie, Cookie Monster, Big Bird and all the rest. Back then in Butchie's childhood, there was Captain Kangaroo, Mr. Rogers and Soupy Sales. All "fags", according to his father. So, he never watched them. He couldn't have his daddy thinking he was a "fag" too. Hell, he didn't even know what a "fag" was. But, it couldn't be anything good.

Butchie and Gracie would pass the hours talking to Big Bird and the rest about the world issues. Gracie didn't make much sense. But she was happy. Butchie was starting to get the hang of this "happy" stuff.

Nichole was not as pretty as her name would imply. In earlier years, Butchie would say that she "barked at the moon". But this was a different chapter in his life. Now she was beautiful, albeit inside. To Nikki, no other man existed in the world, except her Butchie. She cooked beautiful meals. She made love when she was exhausted. To her, that was love. No one had ever treated him this way.

Nikki didn't really get along with her mother. But, the one thing she never forgot was the way her mom took care of Pop. When he walked in the door at night, the day began for Mom. She met him with a fresh drink in her hand. Pop wore slippers. Today, this is a lost tradition. She sat him down, took the ten hours of hard work off his feet, wrapped him in soft slippers and gave him the newspaper. The newspaper, also a lost bit of Americana. Now it's the internet. This was the stuff of storybooks. There would be no Ozzie & Harriet or Archie and Edith, or even Oliver and Jenny, of "Love Story', who could show her a greater love story than the one she saw in front of her everyday.

Fast forward, now Butchie was Nicole's project, the one that she was born to make the drink and fetch the slippers for. He was screaming with need. He was steel. She was the magnet. So, there they were. A nice, tidy little family punctuated by the final pieces—Gracie and George. It didn't matter that the couch was ripped. It didn't matter that Kraft Mac 'n' Cheese was the main course. It didn't matter that their VCR was broken. The only thing that mattered to Nikki was the joy that she felt watching Butchie play with Gracie. The only thing that mattered to Gracie, was Dad's arm around her, as they both tried to follow Big Bird on TV. The only thing that mattered to George . . . . was nothing. George was George, dumb and happy. A tongue looking for a face.

WHEN A GLASS BREAKS

Halloween was around the corner. It was Gracie's first understanding of the fun that came with Halloween. Nikki made a ghost outfit for Trick or Treating. Ghosts were everywhere. The radio played "Monster Mash", by Bobby "Boris" Pickett. The Sesame characters were knee deep in the fun of the season. Gracie couldn't wait for the big night. And then it came. Nikki dressed her little ghost. Butch came home early for the picture taking. Then they would all go out for the fun. Gone were the days of children Trick or Treating alone. Parents were everywhere, showing off their prize winning costumes on their little mannequins and protecting their treasures from the increasing number of low lifes in the world.

The four of them were walking toward their first house. George, of course, had to be part of the fun, though he had no idea of what was going on. To him, it was just an opportunity to slobber all the little faces that were just a bit taller than him. Nikki made a little fedora and sunglasses for George. The glasses lasted less than a block. But, surprisingly, George proudly pranced with his little hat on. In the distance, there was a noise. Kind of a screeching. Butchie heard it. He thought for a split second. A car's tires? Nah, it must be part of a kid's costume, a noise maker.

That was it. It was a monster's screech. George heard it too and there he went. Four clumsy feet and that smile that dogs have, running full speed. Butch yelled, but knew that it was fruitless. George always ran . . . . and George always came back. So, after a weak attempt to run after George, Butch stopped. As he turned around, Gracie passed him right by. Nikki's view was blocked by Butch. They were right at the intersection and Gracie was in the street. Neither one of them saw her.

Butchie turned, frantically. At that instant, he heard a dull thud, coming from down the street. The sound of tires screeching filled the night air, like the flying ghosts and witches of the season.

Then, to his right, he heard another. Butch froze, like a deer in headlights. The horror of the night would take away Butch and Nikki's reason to live.

*"The flying tires, the busted glass, the painful scream that I heard last"* . . . . J. Frank Wilson and The Cavaliers.

But this wasn't a song. It was real life. Say Goodnight Gracie. Goodnight George.

# NINETEEN

RUBY'S HOUSE HAD to be worth at least $8 Million. Twice a year or so, Gene and Geri had to attend a lavish dinner with Ruby, his obnoxious wife and Isaac and his wife, at the Palace. Liberace would have been proud of Ruby's digs.

The conversation was boring. The only thing that made the evening palatable was the music. Ruby liked DooWop. Rather than listen to Ruby and Isaac solve the problems of the world, Gene listened to Dion and The Capris and The Elegants. When he drifted back to reality, the conversation got around to the office. What else. Ruby employed illegal immigrants. A lot of illegal immigrants. He paid them next to nothing and fancied himself a savior. The Rabbis would be proud. "Why should I pay medical expenses and taxes and vacations to some low life to move boxes from here to there, when I can use these dogs?"

Geri agreed with him. Gene was shocked. She had this inate sense that, to survive in Ruby's well paying world, Geri had to keep Ruby happy. She allowed him to kiss her a little too aggressively. She allowed the occasional pat on the ass. Keep the peace. That was her goal. These things never happened in front of Gene.

This time the conversation about the illegals was hot and heavy. Geri was absolutely convincing. By the end of the conversation, she turned to Gene, sitting to her right, and winked. Gene was relieved. She was playing the game. Nobody could be that good, Gene thought. But, she was a charmer.

Toward the end of the evening, the phone rang. The guests never found out who was on the phone. Ruby told the headset, "I figured it was time to give my people a good meal. I pay them too much. Yet they come here and eat my food like it was their last meal". Even if it were a tolerable evening, which it was, the face of every guest went beyond red . . . . purple. Some embarrassed. Some enraged. But the minions let it pass. When it was time to leave, Gene, Isaac and his wife, and Geri stood up as if the Ruby work

~43~

buzzer went off. Geri excused herself and retired to the powder room. When she was finished, she gathered herself, took a little cup from the bathroom and headed for the kitchen.

Ruby fancied himself a discriminating Port wine drinker. Only the most expensive was served at Casa de Rubinstein. Geri poured a snifter halfway with the port. Then she dropped a cup of Geri's finest urine into the glass. Everyone was in the hall, putting on their coats.

"It was a wonderful evening, Ruby", Geri said, as she handed him his drink. "That's my girl, Geri. You always take care of me. What would I do without you", as he slyly patted her ass. "What would you do without Gene" she countered. "Overpaid or not". Ruby took a sip, swirled the rich man's brew around in his mouth and reminded everyone that tomorrow was a work day. 8:00AM sharp. Good night. Good night.

As she closed the door, Geri added . . . . "you ignorant fuck".

# TWENTY

FRIDAYS. GOD, HOW important Fridays had become. Gene and Geri recharged on Fridays. They got lost in each other. First, they had a beautiful dinner by candlelight. Then they made their way down to their sanctuary. It was a Rec Room that was the size of the entire house above. All you could want was there . . . a pool table, a foos ball table, a gym, a bar, and then there was Gene's pride, a juke box. It was loaded with DooWop records. Gene was only twelve when the fifties ended, but DooWop limped along until 1963 or so. It was then that the Beatles, single handedly, massacred the genre. It wasn't as if Gene didn't graduate into the new genre. He still owned many 60's records. He still knew all the Beach Boys songs. But his heart was in the fifties.

They would fire up the juke, and fire up their hearts at the same time. A couple of glasses of wine and soon they were on their own private dance floor. Gene would sing in her ear. It was his return to the street corners of New York. He was a white Frankie Lymon. First tenor voice. Nothing could break their mood on Fridays. Poor Geri had to endure the same stories most Fridays. Gene would tell her of the racism that permeated the music scene back then. "Sh-Boom" was his first example. The best version of that classic was recorded by The Chords, a black group. Soon, the record companies rushed a bunch of pretty white boys into the studio and, out came "Sh-Boom" by The Crewcuts. Hitsville. "Wonderful Girl" was "taken" from The Five Satins and recorded by Dion & The Belmonts. The very emergence of Elvis Presley was due to promoters who capitalized on his recordings of the black rhythm & blues music of the forties and early fifties. His first real attention getter was "Hound Dog". This was a 1953 Blues Classic by Big Momma Thornton. But Big Momma didn't look like Elvis and she certainly wasn't the right color for "Equal Opportunity" America.

Jackie Robinson would agree to that.

But, all these years later, there were Gene and Geri, lost in each others arms, every Friday night. Upstairs, the world could be crumbling like an imploding Vegas Hotel and they wouldn't notice.

The 1974 Seeburg would "stroll" down the track, like a purposeful drill sergeant, and single out the records. The last dance of the evening went to the Bobby Vee hit that was actually another black R&B classic originally done by The Clovers. Gene pulled Geri closer. The intro, then the voice. Gene looked through her eyes and sang.

*"Devil or Angel, I can't make up my mind"*. They were happier than any other time, while they were at their Friday sock hop. Geri looked back at Gene. "I want to be with you forever. If I die first, you'd better come and find me in heaven". "Your family lineage is a whole lot better than mine" Gene said. "I'll be long gone before you. But don't you worry, sweetheart, I'll be there. You can't lose me". The music serenaded them. *"Devil or Angel, dear, whichever you are, I love you, I love you, I love you"*.

# TWENTY ONE

IT WAS A beautiful, crisp Fall day in the middle of September. It was Tuesday and that meant that Gene was heading for Newark Airport for three days of pretending that he loved his job. Their boat would only be in the water for another week, so this particular trip killed Gene to have to take. He and Geri had had a wonderful evening the night before. He was consistent in the attention that he paid to his beautiful wife at their dinner table. It wasn't just a "show" for the road.

But, business beckoned. The drive to the airport was always frenetic. Two hours of nervous anticipation. Will he get there on time? Will the plane be there or enroute from Oshkosh? There was nothing worse than rushing to the airport, only to sit there for two hours, waiting for the plane.

Driving to the airport was always the same. A glance to the left or right revealed another schmo, making his way to his livelihood.

Gene was reminded of a time, thirty years ago, when he was part of a carpool. Long Island, New York. He and three desk jockies were on the Long Island Expressway at the same time every day. They would see the same tired, oblivious faces. One of Gene's crowd was a guy named Larry, who would mumble to himself. Like clockwork, Larry would open his brown paper bag, with his Lunch du Jour, bring the bag up to his eyes, peer into it, and grab the sandwich. He ate his lunch everyday at 7:00AM. This would drive everyone crazy.

Then there was Lenny. Strange dude, indeed. Len always wanted reassurance that everyone liked him. So, he would do crazy things. One morning traffic was moving at the usual 10 mile per hour pace, passing the Route 110 Exit. Sitting in the shotgun seat, Len studied the driver of each car to our right. When he found a guy who was practically asleep and driving on automatic pilot, Len was ready for the attack. He rolled his window down. The paradox was that, 6,000 cars were on the Expressway, yet it was very quiet. Len waited until we were right alongside this guy. At the top of his lungs, Lenny screamed . . . "Hey You!". It's a good thing that the guy he chose didn't have a heart condition. Len would have been the first guy on trial for murder, just for greeting someone. The driver jumped a foot from his 1972 Plymouth Valiant bench seat, hit his head, came down, landed and looked like death. We never laughed so hard as that day.

Now, so many years later, Gene was going to the airport, instead of the office. The car could have driven itself. Same route, same exits. He pulled into the off site parking. It was about 40% cheaper than the Newark rates. Ruby liked that. He got out of the car, checked to see if he had everything, opened the trunk, looked in the glove box, felt his pocket for his wallet. He did this routine three times. Now he was ready to hand the keys to the attendant, who didn't spend much time in school. "When come back" he said. "Thursday". "Bweek?", said the attendant. "What?" "Bweek!" "BUICK", Gene responded. Gave the guy a buck and got on the waiting bus. It was the bus with no springs or shock absorbers. For those, Gene thought, you have to pay extra. He sat alone for five minutes, now getting somewhat impatient. He was two hours early, but he hated every second that went by. Never relaxed until he arrived at the gate. He could see the manager approaching the bus. "Jesus, something must be wrong with the Bweek", he thought.

# TWENTY TWO

"DON'T YOU WANT to see history?" This was too much for Gene at 9:30 AM. He had been up since 5:00AM. "What?" "Come, look". Gene got out of the bus and looked up at the TV that was mounted on the pole. CNN, as always. What he saw didn't quite register at first. A big plane, flying directly into the World Trade Center! "My God", he thought. "This doesn't do much for my confidence this morning." Like a deer, looking at his sling shot back at home, Gene was frozen. Then he must have heard Ruby's voice, snapped out of it. "Hey", he yelled "Let's go, I've got to get over to the airport". The driver, dumb as he was, knew more than Gene at the moment. After a minute, looking like a confused puppy, he hopped into the driver's seat and off they went. Just him and Gene.

The airport was like a ghost town. Incredibly, it emptied out so fast and so soon after this plane crashed. By then, it was not plane, but planes. Now, the thought of an accident was gone. It took Gene a while, but he realized that a catastrophe of unbelievable measure had just taken place. He took on the mindset of one being hunted. Gotta get back to my car. Gotta call my wife. Gotta call my kids. After finding a lone shuttle bus still on the grounds of the airport, he flagged it down, gave the driver a twenty dollar bill to take him back to his car. Attempts to use his cell phone were fruitless. This feeling of helplessness couldn't exist in big, bad America! But there it was.

As he drove out of Newark Airport, he could actually see, at one point, downtown Manhattan. One tower was still standing. Next to it was the biggest smoke cloud he'd ever seen. The other tower was either behind the black blanket or down. The thought of the buildings crumbling had not yet entered his mind. He didn't stop to stare as many did. He pointed the car west on Route 78 and drove like hell, steering wheel in one hand and the cell phone in his other. It wasn't until he was almost to Pennsylvania that he finally had a cell signal.

Reached his wife. Reached his kid's house, but only the answering machine. "Stay in the house" he screamed. He arrived home, hugged Geri and had to lie down. By then, it was about 1PM. At 4:30PM, he woke up. In his warped sense of priority, he called Isaac. Couldn't reach him. He then tried Ruby's cell phone. The call went through. Ruby's unimaginable response, "Did you make the meeting?" At that point, he hated Ruby more than whomever had perpetrated this vicious act of terrorism.

# TWENTY THREE

WHILE ALL THE world was paralyzed by the events of September the 11th, Ruby was putting together plans for Presidents' Day promotions. The plan was to hit the airports and blitz the majors with a road show, presenting low end junk to Kmart, WalMart, Target, BJ's, Costco and every other major account in the country. Was he oblivious to what had just taken place? The week from hell?

On Tuesday the 11th, close to 3,000 people went to work in the Trade Center and The Pentagon. On Tuesday evening, they were gone and the lives of hundreds of thousands who, in some way, shared their lives, even in the smallest way, were affected forever. The next day, New York Mayor Rudy Giuliani predicted that the death toll would be in the thousands. Air travel was resumed on Thursday as the country tried to mimic normalcy. This, while lower Manhattan resembled bombed out cities in Europe during World War II.

On September 11th, people were saying their good byes from their desperate perches high above in the towers. Some had a choice to make . . . . die by fire or jump to their deaths, hoping beyond hope, that they would somehow go "to sleep" before they hit the ground below. It was raining humanity. Others were "luckier". The planes that they took to visit loved ones or to close that big deal took them to Jesus quickly as they met the buildings with full force.

Still others, who were on the other plane, the one in Pennsylvania, went down fighting. They went down with a full understanding of what was happening. They fought. They averted an even bigger calamity and met their maker in what had been a beautiful field just the day before.

51

# TWENTY FOUR

OVER THE NEXT week to two weeks, there was a frantic effort by Policemen, Firemen, Port Authority Officers, civilians, clergy and doctors and nurses. All with one purpose . . . find, transport and save as many brothers and sisters as was possible. Sleep was the enemy. Oxygen tanks replaced hamburgers. The hard, now hallowed, ground replaced their comfortable beds. There was enough adrenaline fueled energy to send a rocket to the moon.

On September 17th, the Taliban, Afghanistan's Islamic extremists, met to decide whether or not to hand over the identified ring leader of the attacks, Osama Bin Laden. America learns from the Press that, on the day of the attacks, when President Bush halted all air travel in the United States, one plane was allowed to fly out of America. It carried the family of the very same Osama Bin Laden. This was never explained.

On September 21st, the Taliban rulers refuse to hand over Bin Laden. Ruby, a man who prays every morning, puts all this aside. There's business to do. There's junk to sell. Gene and Isaac are in the office everyday, with one ear to the television for the day's events.

# TWENTY FIVE

ALTHOUGH HE IS a professional Sales Manager, Gene escapes his pragmatism by writing and singing. Because of his long commute, he stays at a local hotel near the office. On one reflective night, Gene pens a poem. It was a way for him to release pain, frustration and, in some way, convince himself that he was in control of what was going on around him.

Any New York sports junkie knows that when (not if, but when), a New York team wins a World Championship, they are treated to a ticker tape parade in the downtown Manhattan financial district. The parade route has become known as the Canyon of Heroes.

# CANYON OF HEROES

THERE WERE PINSTRIPES EVERYWHERE,
ON KIDS OF EVERY AGE,
THEY WERE STRETCHING FOR A PEEK,
AT THEIR FAVORITE PLAYER'S FACE.

DOWN THE BLACKTOP CAME THE CARS,
IN THE SHADOWS OF "THE WALL",
HIGH AS YOU CAN SEE,
CANYON OF HEROES, AS IT'S CALLED.

EVERYWINDOW IN THE WALL,
FILLED, LIKE BLEACHERS AT THE YARD,
THEY WERE CHEERING ON THE CHAMPS,
GOD, THEY PLAYED SO HARD.

AT SHORT, OUR BOY WAS FAST.
THE CATCHER, TOUGH AS NAILS,
BOY, OUR PITCHERS MOWED 'EM DOWN,
OUR GUYS REALLY WHIPPED THEIR TAILS.

BUT TO GET TO REACH THIS PLACE,
IT TOOK ONE HEROIC DASH.
ONE HUNDRED EIGHTY FEET,
FROM SECOND TO THE CASH.

THE BALL WAS BOUNCING EVERYWHERE,
FIRST JUGGLED IN LEFT FIELD,
THEN THE THROW TO SHORT WAS DROPPED,
PAST THIRD NOW, OUR BOY HAD WHEELS.

THE THROW WAS HIGH, THE SLIDE WAS LOW,
THE DUST WAS EVERYWHERE,
WHEN ALL HAD STOPPED, OUR BOY LOOKED UP
TO SEE IF HE WAS FAIR.

ED RENNER

THERE WAS CHAOS EVERYWHERE,
AND FEAR ON HIS YOUNG FACE.
THE FIREMAN LOOKED UP,
NO MORE TOWERS, EMPTY SPACE.

DOWN THE BLACKTOP RAN HIS TROOPS,
IN THE SHADOWS OF "THE WALL",
PEOPLE RUNNING TO ESCAPE,
THE CANYON HEROES TOWARD THE FALL.

EVERY CAMERA SHOWED THE WORLD,
THE COURAGE THESE MEN HAVE.
CLAWING THROUGH THE DIRT,
LOOKING BLINDLY FOR A "SAVE".

THERE WAS DANGER EVERYWHERE,
LIKE CRAWLING THROUGH A VICE,
BUT AS LONG AS THERE WAS HOPE,
THERE WAS THEM, DAMN THE PRICE!

THE WALL WAS BEATING THEM,
THEY WERE LOSING HEROES FAST,
TWO HUNDRED PLUS WERE LOST,
TO THE UNFORGIVING BLAST.

THEY WALKED BACK DOWN THE STREETS,
THE CROWD STRETCHING FOR A PEEK,
AT THESE TIRED "EVERYMEN"
TOO TIRED TO EVEN SPEAK.

NOW THE CANYON HAS ANOTHER GUEST,
THESE FIREMEN SO BRAVE,
PLEASE LET US FIND ANOTHER LIFE,
THE CROWD LOOKED UP AND PRAYED.

WHEN A GLASS BREAKS

# TWENTY SIX

GENE WAS A kid who grew up just a mile or so north of the World Trade Center. In better times, he had remembered those parades held in the very same neighborhood on the very same streets where bodies landed. The parades celebrated a Championship won by this team or that team from New York. This was where their heroism was acknowledged. This was where people looked out the windows and cheered . . . . and danced. Some of the same people looked out the same windows on September 11th and saw people dropping out of the sky to their deaths. Canyon of Heroes now took on an entirely different meaning.

That night, sitting at the mini desk in the budget hotel, Gene's pen kept going as if he were firing bullets of frustration rather than words.

# THREE LADIES AND A KING
## (THE NEW YORK BOMBING DISASTER)

WHEN HE STARED AT THE TV,
AND SAW THE BUILDINGS AND THE FLAMES,
THE LITTLE BOY CRIED,
FOR IT WAS REAL.

HE WAS SCARED, HE WONDERED WHY,
CLUTCHED HIS MOTHER, BEGAN TO SHAKE.
THE LADY'S KNEE BENT,
AND THEN SHE KNEELED.

HELP US THROUGH THIS, DEAR FATHER,
HELP US UNDERSTAND
HOW THEY DO THIS IN YOUR NAME,
HOW THEY CALL IT "HOLY LAND".

WHEN SHE SAW IT FROM HER PERCH,
SAW THE BUILDING AND THE FLAMES,
THE STATUE "WEPT",
AS IF SHE WERE REAL.

SHE HAD "SEEN" SO MANY THINGS,
BLESSED THIS HARBOR, WELCOMED ALL.
THIS LADY STOOD STILL,
WE WERE STILL FREE.

HELP ME THROUGH THIS, DEAR FATHER,
THOUGH I DO NOT LIVE,
THEY LOOK TO ME FOR FREEDOM,
IT'S ALL I HAVE TO GIVE.

WHEN SHE LOOKED DOWN FROM HEAVEN,
SAW THE KILLING AND THE SIN,
OUR HOLY MOTHER CRIED,
"THEY MOCK MY SON".

WHEN A GLASS BREAKS

HE HAD DIED FOR ALL THEIR SINS,
GAVE US SANCTIFYING GRACE,
"MY KING OF KINGS,
WHAT HAVE THEY DONE".

HELP THEM THROUGH THIS, DEAR FATHER,
TEACH THEM HOW TO LIVE,
GIVE THOSE WHO'VE LOST THEIR LOVED ONES,
THE POWER TO FORGIVE.

# TWENTY SEVEN

FORTUNATELY FOR GENE, unfortunately for Ruby, there would be no traveling for the foreseeable future. Even if he could get out of town, buyers weren't buying. Meetings were put off. So the evening was spent at home with Geri. It was Wednesday, or maybe Thursday, of the week after 9-11. A scotch on the rocks, a dance to one of the tunes from the juke box and then some TV made up the evening. The CNN News was horrific. Interviews with one grieving family after another. Desperate to find Dad or Mom or Uncle Joe, people made their way to the neighborhood near the World Trade Center, now known as Ground Zero. "Who came up with that one?", Gene complained. "Why do we have to name everything?"

It was agonizing television. One after another, they stood before the camera, holding pictures. Have you seen my father? Please look for my Mom. The pain on the faces could tear the viewer apart. We heard life stories that were, in fact, life stories. Grandpa Al was kind to everyone. Sister Mary Kate was an angel on this earth. Occasionally there was anger. FIND MY BROTHER!

The News media did what they always do. Report anything. Don't worry about accuracy. Get a story out first. We can correct the story later, at 3:00AM, when nobody's watching. *Could make you sick,* Gene thought. One reporter was smart enough to figure out that there was a Day Care Center in the bowels of the building complex. Dead children. That'll sell a lot of the sponsor's toothpaste.

Geri gasped. She started to cry, uncontrollably. Later we found out the truth. 28 children were saved, thanks to the quick thinking of the Center's Executive director, Charlene Melville. This feat was recognized with an award from the Governor's Office on September 12th. But, this news of the heroism . . . . of the safe children . . . . of the Governor's award, didn't reach the public for quite a while. It was better press that children perished at the hands of the terrorists.

"Oh my God, little children" cried Geri.

# TWENTY EIGHT

DENNIS MCGAFF WAS the company gopher. Go for this Dennis, go for that, Dennis. None of it seemed to bother him. When the clock struck five, he was out the door heading home to his family. He was the most devoted husband and father that Gene had ever met.

To his neighbors, Dennis was the volunteer fireman, who saved the kid down the block. To his friends, he was the weakest bowler on the Friday night team, with the biggest smile. To Father Joseph, he was the most dependable Altar "Boy", although he was over forty years old. To all who knew him, Dennis was a special human being.

Yet, to his co-workers at Ruby's sweat shop, Dennis was a glorified mail clerk, with the courage of a flea.

Every morning, Dennis knocks on the open door in Gene's office. Same every morning . . . "Remem mem mem re mem ma member. Morning Gino! What's the flip side of Blue Moon?" "Goodbye To Love"

"Goddamnit. One day I'm going to get you." "Never happen" Gene responded. At that moment, the screeching voice of Hatman resonated over the loud speaker . . . . *Dennis McGaff, NOW!* The melodic tones of Ruby and The Fabulous Intercoms.

"Why do you put up with this shit?" Gene asked him. "I don't really know. I'm 46. I'm not going to be the President of AT&T. The job is close to my house. I shoot pool 3 nights a week at Kelly's Bar. It's not a bad life." Three nights a week Dennis would get plastered. There were days that he was nowhere to be found when the office opened. Ruby kept him around because Dennis was his lap dog. He didn't pay him much. Tonight was Kelly's pool tournament. Dennis wouldn't be seen for the next three days.

# TWENTY NINE

I T WAS ONLY days after the buildings went down. The dead were still under the rocks that used to be paychecks for the thousands. The television news reports were sobering. First, the buildings getting hit. Then the angry, relentless gray cloud chasing people down the street. Then the sight of the "gray people" wandering the street as if lost. Walking statues.

Reporters hit the streets by day and were ready for the 11:00PM News. As Gene and Geri watched, he was old enough to remember the 11:00PM News in the sixties. Every show started with the day's dead count in VietNam. Of course, the Americans always outkilled the VietNamese. So, why weren't we winning? Gene would ask the 19" screen every night. All these years later, the story was the same. The difference now was that it wasn't the reporter telling the story. It was real people begging to the camera, holding a picture of their loved one.

"Please, if you've seen my dad, my mom, my husband, call this number. He (she) worked on the 88th floor in Tower One. If you see him (her) walking the streets, call this number."

Tears. Real tears. One after another, these walking victims. Begging. All who watched TV at night were introduced to the dead. They became their families. They became their priests and nuns and ministers and rabbis, praying for these people that they didn't even know, yet they were their own fathers and mothers and brothers and sisters. They were all united as one. The irony is that everyone was praying to the same God that these terrorists were trying to impress. Sick.

Frightened moms were facing the prospects of raising the little children in their arms by themselves. At the sight of a young mom clutching her three year old, Geri started to shake. Gene took her in the solace of his arms. It was no help. She began to cry.

"It was a dog" she murmered. "It was a dog".

Gene thought she saw a dead dog lying on the street during the TV Report. "Put it out of your mind" Gene said. "No, it was a dog. It had to be a dog! Why did I leave?"

At that point, Gene found out that he didn't quite know everything about his angel.

Geri unwrapped her story in unison with the latest victim on the screen. She was driving home from work. It was around 6:00PM on a soon to be dark October evening some years ago. She was driving just a bit over the limit, when she spotted a car to her left as she approached an intersection. She had the green light, but it looked like that car wasn't going to stop. Look at the road, look at that car. Look at the road, look at the car. Two missiles wanting the same space. The guy made an unusual zig zag. Geri thought for sure the guy was drunk. The car blew the light but made a high speed turn to the right, almost hitting her. The road in front of Geri was the furthest thing from her mind. Then, a thump. *Jesus, I hit something.* It was dark now. Through her rear view mirror, she saw something. A dog, maybe. It wasn't moving. Geri floored the pedal, making an electric quick decision. When she arrived home, she poured a Scotch on the rocks. Geri didn't even drink. She was cold sober, but in a drunken haze. The TV was on, but it was as if she were dreaming. The handsome anchor man's voice was coming from some distance. "A child was killed by a hit and run driver tonight at the intersection of . . . . Geri never heard the full report. She turned out the lights, turned off the TV and sat in the dark, like a sinner in a confessional box. A second drink and a third. In the eerie silence of her room, only one sound broke the darkness. "It was a dog . . . it was a dog".

It was an awakening for Gene. Now, he knew why she never wanted to drive. Now, he knew why she screamed at him when he would arrive home and instantly make a drink. A drink to wash away the stench of Ruby. "Geri, sweetheart, we live in a big city. There are many streets and many accidents every day. You aren't an idiot. You're an intelligent, lucid woman. I'm sure that you are right. It was a dog. Thank God that lunatic didn't hit you on his turn. For all you know, it was his car that hit the dog."

To the sound of another grieving dad and to the site of walking gray people, she could feel herself drifting into a sleep. "Good night sweetheart" "Good night Gene". The safe silence of the next two minutes was broken. "It was a dog".

Excerpts from "Who Asked?"

There is only one Bill Clinton. Of course, there are many Bill Clintons in the world. But there is only one Bill Clinton, former President of the United States (thank God). So, where did the expression come from when a reporter, or anybody really, refers to the "Bill Clintons of the world" when they want to make a point. Or, the John Gottis of the world! Where did this come from?

A person eats healthful food and it helps him to be healthy. It is the person, who is healthy, not the food! Geez!

Farther means distance. Further means a continuance of a point.

Is there anyone out there, who would purchase a box of tea because it's The Official Tea of The Imus In The Morning Program? Or buy a car because it's "The Official Car of the New York Mets"? This is old advertising jargon whose time has come and gone. Same with "That's Right"! As if people hang on every word of a commercial and speak to the commercial, saying, "No, really"? Stupid!

Asterisk, not asterik!

Excerpts from "Who Asked?" (cont'd)

A team is a collective word designating, as a unit, a group of people. You say . . . a team. You say . . . four teams. So, why do the idiot sports announcers misuse another term, RBI? An RBI is an abbreviation for Run Batted In. When a batter drives in one runner, he is credited with AN RBI. If he drives in 3 runners, he is credited with THREE RBI'S (RBI being a unit). The genius' who are too smart for their own good, have taken to calling it 3 RBI! You don't say 3 TEAM! Why 3 RBI? Geez!

Gene has spoken. Angry Gene has spoken.

# THIRTY

GROUND ZERO FLOODED the news. Devastated people carried pictures, begging the news cameras to find their loved ones. This didn't matter to Ruby. Hell, he didn't lose any of his family. "Where's the orders" he would screech. Somehow, it didn't occur to him that people weren't interested in going to their local WalMart to buy a sixty dollar cassette player for their car. If the term didn't already belong to the Buddy Holly legacy, September 11th could very well had been the day the music died.

Ruby would have none of it. The voice that made everyone cringe screamed over the intercom system. "Product meeting in my office in ten minutes"! "Dennis McGaff, call . . . . NOW"! Another torture session, no doubt.

Piece count. Ruby's marketing strategy was to throw ten things into a styrofoam inner box next to the Cassette player and present the collection as a Bonus Buy. Free this and free that, just for buying this relic car stereo. Gene was amazed that this strategy actually worked. The low end consumer liked getting all this free stuff. Gene had even "invented" a product that was hugely successful. It was dubbed Road Rider Series. A radio, a flashlight, an accident reflector and a tape of a Willie Nelson album called, what else, On The Road Again. Gene, who had come to Ruby's company from the real audio industry, felt like he had sold his soul representing junk like this.

But there was Ruby, throwing ideas out in rapid fire fashion. Let's put this with this or that with this. When all this craziness ended, Gene and Isaac had ten items to carry to the Mass Merchants.

People were still lying dead beneath tons of steel and Ruby (and The Fabulous Frank Lloyd Wrights) was playing product designer. Designer Junk, a new category.

Like a football huddle after the quarterback finishes calling the play, he barks . . . on two, break! Ruby, trying to endear himself, issued the same command in the same cadence. Everybody laughed. Under their breaths, they all had the same thought . . . . SCHMUCK!

Now it was time to build these product kits. These ground breaking new products. Ruby picked up his phone, dialed the intercom. "Dennis McGaff, call, NOW!" His CFO, also his Office Manager, personnel man and chief cheer leader, Norman, said "Dennis is out again". This is the third day. Another drunken stupor, Ruby thought. "He's fired. Fire him. This is the last time" Ruby was ranting. His eyes were red and slightly wet. "He's fired. That's it, he's fired"!

As Gene witnessed this melt down, all he could think of was tomorrow morning. Before he comes to work, Ruby prays for an hour behind close doors. Gene recalled the song lyrics from the sixties song, Eve of Destruction. *"Hate your next door neighbor, but don't forget to say Grace".*

# THIRTY ONE

ACROSS THE HUDSON, a horrific gravesite. Eve of Destruction indeed, thought Gene.

Gene and Geri were having dinner. Thankfully, and not surprisingly, Gene's big presentation had been cancelled. For a while, there didn't seem to be anything to do at the office, but talk to buyers and salespeople all over the country about September 11th, now known as 911. The feeling from places as far away as the company's suppliers in China was that *all* people in the area were victims.

Fresh swordfish was on the menu this particular evening. It was one of Gene's favorites. Gerri loved it for a different reason. It was easy to make. A few spices, a lot of time marinating and bingo.

Add rice, another easy preparation and the result was the best excuse to sip a good Chardonnay that there could be. Small talk filled the air. The TV light competed with the single candle on the table for their attention. The ambience was enhanced by one of Gene's home made CD's. No doowop here. Dinner was more "Sardi's". Johnny Mathis, Sinatra, Vivaldi . . . In the background was the TV sound at a very low volume.

As usual, the news was the dead count of the day. It seemed such an irony to have the TV on during a romantic dinner. But, Gene would have felt, somehow, unpatriotic, if he didn't have the news going.

The scene switched to the now famous chain linked fence. It was the one with the flowers and the prayer cards covering every available inch. Standing in front of the fence were tonight's desperate searchers. "Please, dad, I know you are watching. Wherever you are, call us and we'll come get you". One after another, these people, now soul mates, filled the screen. Tears on the screen. Tears in Gene and Geri's Dining room. As if an eerie message, Sinatra is in the background, singing "Come fly with me, let's fly, let's fly away". It was as if The Chairman of the Board knew that many folks had indeed flown as they jumped from the buildings, choosing this fate instead of fire.

The camera panned left to right, giving everyone their two minutes. Heart wrenching pictures. Words barely audible over the crying. Constant camera movement. Conversation accompanied the meal. Small talk, mostly. Occasionally, they would glance at the screen. A young girl, a child herself, holding her child and talking to the camera which had transformed itself into her husband's beautiful blue eyes, now probably closed. Geri saw the girl, saw the child and broke down. Unstoppable tears. Gene understood. And didn't. And comforted her until she calmed down.

The camera moved on as if waiting for Geri to stop crying. There on the screen was an unshaven, shabbily dressed man. He, also, was holding a picture. Conversation stopped in the dining room. Eyes focused on this man, who looked as though he hadn't had a shower in over a week.

"My God, Geri, it's Dennis McGaff".

Dennis was holding a picture of his pride, his New York City fireman son. Unlike the others, Dennis couldn't find words. It was as if he knew that the words would fall on dead ears. Gene repeated "It's Dennis McGaff".

September 11th just got personal. Gene repeated, "Dennis fuckin' McGraff".

A few people from the office saw Dennis on TV. The telephone chain started. Gene already had two calls into Ruby's house. No answer. The next morning, Gene didn't wait until he got to the office.

He was right back on the phone to Ruby's house. This time, there was an answer. Mrs. Lopez was the maid, probably an illegal. Ruby paid her nothing. She was happy for the job. A match made in heaven. Meester Rubenstein is saying hees prayers, Meester Shanahan. Can I give heem the message?

When Gene told her about Dennis, he could hear her response . . . "Dios Mio" and he could see her make the sign of the cross, right through his telephone. "I will tell him, Meester Shanahan".

It was no surprise that Ruby never called Gene back. At the office, when Ruby finally arrived, Gene was sitting outside Ruby's office. Gene was still a pale white. Ruby looked like he had just come from the local tanning salon. Like a minion, Gene followed him into the marble dressed office. And he told Ruby.

"I know" said Hatman. "Norman called me". As if he were purposely reciting a run on sentence, Gene spoke. "You have to give Dennis his job back, we have to help him, we have to call his family, we have to take up a collection . . . ."

Ruby, patiently or impassionately, said the unimagineable.

WHEN A GLASS BREAKS

"I can't help it that this happened. I didn't do it. I didn't fly the planes. Dennis should have been here. He couldn't do anything to find his son anyway". Gene left speechless. God forgive him for what was going on in his mind.

# THIRTY TWO

THE BODY OF young Patrick McGaff was found. He had been in the "still standing" second tower lobby. Paddy, as Dennis would proudly call him, had spotted an older woman near the newspaper stand. She was motionless, as if the horror of the day had screwed her legs into the ground. Paddy and his partner ran toward her. They lifted her, ignoring her objections, onto McGaff's shoulders since he was the bigger of the two. The revolving doors were just ahead. Patrick's partner was ahead. He moved much faster, since he didn't have the dead, unwilling weight of the woman to deal with.

His partner flew through the doors and was now out among the running "gray people". Patrick was twenty feet from freedom when he heard a tremendous cracking noise. It sounded like a lost bolt of lightning trapped in the confines of the huge lobby and looking for an escape. He looked up and saw a beam flying right toward him. He uttered his last words . . . "Oh my God".

# THIRTY THREE

"DIOS MIO" CRIED Rosie, in her broken English. Word of Dennis's son's death traveled as fast as the plane that had hit the building. All she could think of was that she should make extra coffee for this more somber than usual morning. There was a silence through the entire office broken only, it seemed, by four calls to Ruby's office. It was Dennis. Tough, loud, obnoxious Ruby wouldn't take his call. He instructed Isaac to tell Dennis that he had been discharged from the company.

In his usual, non-confrontational tone, Dennis told a pale white Isaac that he understood. His last words to Isaac, on the phone . . . "It's OK, Isaac". And he was gone.

That night, Gene called Dennis's home. Mrs. McGaff, a strong lady who could hide her feelings behind her usual caked on makeup, answered the phone. Gene said hello and couldn't find his next words. Seeing this, Geri grabbed the phone. She had the usual "girl talk" and offered to bring over food. Who can eat, Gene thought. By then, he was composed. The phones transferred to Dennis and Gene.

"How are you holding up big guy", Gene asked. "I'm OK, I guess . . . a little numb".

"Dennis, ya gotta get through this. The guy upstairs has a plan for all of us. I know what it feels like to lose a son."

"I know" I'm OK really. Tell everyone in the office that we thank them for their prayers." A long, uncomfortable pause. It seemed like an hour but was probably five or six seconds. Dennis searched his beautiful heart for the strength to find something to say. Something that would calm Gene and, in turn, calm himself. "Hey, who sang "Devil or Angel"? "First the Clovers, then Bobby Vee", said Gene, gratefully. "Yeah right", Dennis whispered. "Bye Gino".

# THIRTY FOUR

AT THE CLOSE of business on Wednesday, the 19th of September, the stock market closed down by 144.27 (1.62%) to 8,759. It was the lowest point since the 1930's. On Friday, the 21st, Congress approved a bill to financially prop up the airlines and also to establish a federal victims fund.

Demonstrations are conducted by tens of thousands in Pakistan against the government's cooperation with the United States. An American of Yemeni descent is fatally shot. Ali Al Mansouri, 44, killed by an angry, ugly American.

By Monday, the 24th, the number of people feared missing was at 6,453. Only 276 were found and identified. The next morning wasn't a holiday on anybody's calendar. Rosh Hashannah started on the 17th and had concluded. It wasn't Thanksgiving or Christmas. Yet no one came to work for Ruby that day. It was something of a walkout in memory of young Paddy and in support of Dennis. The sadness was thicker than a London fog.

Ruby made sure he was on vacation in Aruba living the good life. There would be a Fireman's funeral on Saturday afternoon. One could envision Ruby, on his knees, in his wind swept Aruba Hotel room. Praying. Praying! Praying? Hopefully, this evil crumb of humanity had some prayers for Dennis and Patrick. Gene could only think of one of his father's expressions . . . ." You ain't worth the powder it takes to blow you to hell".

In the next few days, Gene spent a lot of time in church. He would just sit in the quiet church alone, thinking, questioning, denying his faith and calling upon his God to make it all clear to him. On Saturday morning, September 22nd, the funeral was held for Patrick. The room had more flowers than the average flower shop. Where there weren't flowers, there were flags.

Gene and Geri arrived and were shocked to find that the next two rooms were also occupied by 911 victims. One, like Paddy, was a fireman. The other, an accountant, who had the misfortune of having an appointment in the World Trade Center that day. It was a different wake than any Gene had ever attended. The faces were wet with tears. But there was an equal number of people whose faces were wrapped in rage. How could these animals impact a small town like theirs? How could they lose these people? And how could they lose their innocence and their sense of security?

In the worst of times, some unlikely people gain strength as if it were pumped into their bodies just to get them through the crisis. Mrs. McGaff was such a person. She sat, extended her arm to all who visited her to express their condolences. She never cried. Oftentimes, *she* consoled *them*! This kind of strength can never be explained. In contrast, Dennis sat next to her and never raised his eyes from the floor.

Gene never really knew Mrs. McGaff. Dennis was a very private man. But, he thought to himself, what a lucky man Dennis was to have been married to her.

# THIRTY FIVE

GERI HAD DRIVEN to the Funeral Home. It was the first time, in a very long time, that she had driven. "I'll drive home", she said. Gene didn't realize that he was crying like a baby. Probably because everyone was. Geri was too full of rage to cry.

Halfway home they were on the Parkway doing 45 miles per hour. It was as though everyone was in a trance. Geri was screaming at every car she passed. Gene didn't notice. He was miles away, like he was hypnotized. Having reached her boiling point, she floored the pedal and went to the slow lane, pedal down. It was white knuckle driving. Geri was out of control. "All these deaths, all these deaths! All these families! The children! Oh my God, the children!"

Up ahead, an equally impatient driver was moving into the slow lane. Geri was going too fast. "Car, Geri" Gene studdered. Car! It was closer now and Geri could see two images in that car, a little girl, looking out her window. And a dog. Geri pumped the pedal frantically. Her eyes were big, like they were swollen. She pumped the pedal. The car went faster. She was on the gas pedal. "The brake, Geri, hit the brake pedal!" It was as though her leg couldn't move. She knew she had been pumping the gas pedal but she couldn't move. Gene tried to turn the wheel. Better to hit the guard rail. But Geri's grip on the wheel was as strong as Mrs. McGaff's grip on her emotions. It was a direct hit.

The noise and the fire were in step. After what seemed like an hour, the cars all came to a stop. The lights went out. It was all so fast.

Slow. Gene was hanging upside down, the seat belt clinging to him as if he were it's protector. He was groggy and everything now seemed to be moving in slow motion. Someone was moaning. Maybe it was him. He tried to focus. Where was Geri? He looked around the cabin and she wasn't there. Then he was out cold.

# THIRTY SIX

"FASTER", SOMEONE YELLED. This woke him from his trance. The gurney, that he was now laying on, was moving as frantically as the car was just before impact. His functions were still moving at half speed, while the gurney was doing double time. Bang Bang! The swinging doors of the Emergency Room surrendered on impact. Around three turns, two gurneys were flying. He looked up and caught a glimpse. Geri was in the first one. He couldn't focus. Didn't know if she was moving. Again, he heard moaning. This time the pain told him that it was coming from him. He seemed to be outside his body observing the chaos.

Now side by side, the two chariots were in the same room. At once there were doctors and nurses swarming all over him, like pigeons to bread crumbs. He slipped into unconsciousness, but could hear their voices. "We're losing her!" Then he couldn't hear. Then he could. "Stat!" "Clear". Again, "Clear". All different voices with speaking parts, as if they were performers in a play. But this was real. Then quiet.

All he could see was a big light and the masked heads of three doctors. All he could hear was the screaming and the machines. Beep Beep Beep. The voices intensified. The Beeps went faster. The voices louder! The Beeps faster and louder! Then a long Beeeeeep. His beep . . . . or Geri's?

# THIRTY SEVEN

"911, WHAT'S YOUR emergency"

"911, is someone there? What's your emergency"?

A shrill noise, like a wounded bird. "Are you hurt. Where are you calling from"

"He's gonna like this" the voice said. A man's voice, now clearer. "Where are you calling from. This is no joke"

"Yes, it's a joke" And he's gonna like my joke. Because now, I have him"

"Sir, don't hurt anyone. We can talk about this."

"He was the best damned son a man could ever expect to have".

"Sir, whatever he did to you, he's still your son. Put him on the phone, sir. Let's talk about this". This, while the operator was scribbling frantically on paper. *Get me a negotiator. Fast.*

"And now, he's gone".

"Sir, what did you do to him? Is he hurt?" *Trace the number.*

"Sir, tell me about your son. Is he OK? We can help him. Where are you sir? I have two sons. We can help you. Where does he go to school?"

The negotiator was red, in contrast to the color of Paddy, one of the gray people when he died. Gray—the color of the last few days, like the hated visiting team at the stadium. People were scurrying around the 911 Crisis Call Center. Yet, everyone was totally focused. All the while, they were listening to Dennis over the speaker.

"Letter 6" *Serial Killer?, one of them wrote.*

The scurried faces grew more intense, more focused. *Letter 6 is "F". Check for murders of people with names "A" through "F"!*

"Sir, how many are we talking about. Are you mad at a lot of people? We can talk about this, sir. Stay with me. Don't hurt nobody. You sound like a nice man. You don't want to do anything you'll regret."

The wounded bird spoke again . . . . "Fire".

*Check the files . . . . Arson! "Fire" begins with "F".*

"Sir, who are we talking about here? Are there others, besides your son?"

"He was the best damned Fireman in Ladder Company 6. And he's gone. And we're supposed to be selling radios."

The operator, now with something to work with, something different, is frantically waving to the other "911's". Post it notes were flying. *Ladder 6! Ladder 6? Where the fuck is Ladder 6?*

"Sir, stay with me. Don't hurt nobody. My brother's a Firefighter down there at the towers. Are you talking about the towers? Is your son down there?"

A loud, dragging noise interferred the frantic exchange. Then a thud. "Sir, don't be hurting no one. What was that noise". "It's the sound of a door closing. Today a door is going to close"

The tracing equipment was experiencing tremendous technical problems, thanks to the 19 madmen from God. The operators were operating with one hand behind their backs.

From the other side of the room, one of the 911's screamed and whispered at the same time. "It's down the shore. The guy's in Seaside Heights. Ladder 6 is in Seaside Heights. They lost a man down at the towers. Paddy McGaff. His father's name is Dennis."

"Dennis, is that you? Said the operator. There was a pause. "Dennis, we can help you. We can save you. Don't do nothin' stupid."

"Somebody should make him pay. Why does Paddy die and this lowlife get to live? Somebody should fuck with his life. I'm gonna ruin his day. I'm gonna fuck with his life today".

"Dennis, it's been a bad time for all of us. Who are you talking about?" No response. Then . . . "I'm gonna fuck with his life".

The 911's are frantically making calls. "Keep him talking" "For Chrissake, keep him talking. We're close"

"Where are you, Dennis?"

"Garage. Somebody should make him pay."

The call was dispatched. Local cops are racing to Dennis' house. They all knew him. Bowling buddies, fishing club guys and loyal patrons at Kelly's Bar.

Three cars arrive at once. The house was dark. Not a light on in the place, like the grave that would be Paddy's home forever. First a knock at the door. Then, no waiting. The cops broke the door down. No one home.

They raced to the garage, bang on the door. "There's a window on this side" "Break the fuckin' thing"

The electric garage door opens. One of the cops inside the house got to the switch. Like a curtain rising on a tragedy, it lumbers to rise, ever so slowly. Cops on both sides of the opening, guns drawn. They peer in. No cars there. No Dennis either.

# THIRTY EIGHT

"**I**SAAC, CALL ME. NOW!"

Ruby wants to have a meeting about the new line. He sits behind his marble desk, completely oblivious to the Country's tragedy. "Why aren't the Reps returning calls? We have no orders!"

"You fucking idiot, do you have any heart inside that body of yours? Are you aware what's happening in the world?" It was Isaac's voice.

"I didn't fly the planes. I can't help what's happening. I can't put steak on your table unless you put steak on mine. It was his favorite saying. We have work to do".

Isaac lunged at Ruby and landed a punch straight to his face. "There's your steak, you fuck". Ruby, at that moment, transformed into a little boy, who had just been told that he can't have any more dessert. A hurt look. A helpless look. This was not a look that would come from a man who owns a business and is responsible for the livelihood of 50 employees and their families. This was the look of a boy wanting his blankey.

"I want you out of here immediately" Ruby speaks through the new space between his teeth. Tears welled in his eyes. "When I come in tomorrow, I want to see your office empty. And you can call Gene, wherever he is, and tell him he's fired too!"

Of course, Ruby knew that it was Gene, not himself, who had all the relationships with the buyers.

# THIRTY NINE

EAL, NEW JERSEY. How ironic a name. This one town was replete with business owners. In the Consumer Electronics business, it was a "who's who". Four or five of the top retail chains were owned by someone from that community.

The pretty streets were lined with trees. They may as well have been closeout circulars. That was the only beauty these self made thieves understood. The streets were littered with Temples and even a few churches. Mostly Temples. These were the places where they could go to make the instantaneous transition to good people. The place that would convince them that the world was a better place with them in it.

Each of these entrepreneurs knew the other's business. Each took turns being the hero of the day if he turned a quick deal or if he put one over on Uncle Sam.

Ruby drove through the streets, on his way home. This time, he took the back way to his Taj. Nobody should see his swollen mouth. Nobody should see him as anything but a king, a conqueror. In truth, all these men were weak bullies, hiding behind the trigger of a buck.

He turned into his driveway, which had more marble flanking it than the Vatican. The family was in Aruba. He was to join them this weekend. The community did their "cleansing" in Aruba. He always took great pride in his beautiful fortress made, brick by brick, from the sweat of the "lessers". *I can't help it if I'm smarter than them.*

A push of a button in his car and he turned the lights on in the house. A push of another button disengaged the Security System. As he pressed, the light wouldn't go off. There would be hell to pay when he saw his wife. *She never activated the alarm!* Now the garage door slid up. Slowly, just like the poor people's doors. He eased the car into the garage. Something blocked him. The sun in his eyes, as he drove in, clouded his vision. He could just see a form. Got out of the car, cursing his children. Walked around to the front of the car. Even his battered eye opened. He screamed like a woman. There was Dennis McGaff, lying triumphantly on the floor. With a bullet in his head.

# FORTY

GENE WOKE UP. It was very bright, yet he could see nothing. He tried, frantically, to piece together some semblance of reasoning. "Where am I?" Was he speaking or thinking? A voice, maybe his, bellowed, "Geri's gone". Geri's gone. How could this be happening?

Gene closed his eyes for, it seemed hours, but it was only five minutes. He remembered her instructions to him. If she ever went before him, he must find her in heaven.

He was moving, although he didn't know how, and he didn't know where he was going. Just white halls was all he saw. But now he could hear music. Beautiful, happy music.

Then, he was there. And he couldn't believe his eyes . . . . or his mind . . . . or his soul.

# FORTY ONE

## *HEAVEN*

CATHOLICS GENERALLY BELIEVE that Michael the Archangel carries the souls to Heaven. And that Christ gave the keys to Heaven to Peter. Now St. Peter, according to Catholics, a man generally thought to be the first Pope, came to be known as the keeper of the Pearly Gates, the entrance into Heaven.

The buildings of The World Trade Center were destroyed in the name of God, referred to as Allah by extremists, who would portray themselves as protectors of the world, as it should be, according to Allah. The perpetrators of this murderous act carried out the bloodshed in the name of the Islam beliefs.

Heaven in Islam is similar to the heaven of the belief of Judaism and Christianity. The Qur'an, verse 35 of Surah Al-Ra'd, states : The parable of the garden which the righteous are promised. Beneath it flow rivers. Perpetual is the fruits thereof and the shade therein. This is the end for the righteous. For the non believers, the end is Fire, for all eternity.

The planes delivered the Fire. The ironic part of this heinous plan is that it is believed that 350 Muslims died in The World Trade Center.

# FORTY TWO

I N FRONT OF Gene, spinning ever so slowly, was a huge carousel, the size of six hundred Titanics. People were sitting on real animals and the Carousel was rotating, ever so slowly.

My God, Gene thought! Is this Heaven? And why not, he reasoned. He had led a very good life. It was just surrounded by bad. And why shouldn't heaven be a Carousel? There was nothing on Earth that was quite so happy as a beautiful Carousel, nestled in a glorious park.

In the center of the massive Carousel was a stage. There, he saw Buddy Holly. "*Everyday, it's a getting' closer, going faster than a roller coaster, love like yours will surely come my way*"

Next came James Sheppard, of Shep and The Limelites, one of Gene's favorites. How ironic that James and his group were singing "Daddy's Home". Home indeed, being sung by none other than a sheppard.

Gene sat for a while. Next to take the stage was a little boy. My God, Gene thought. It's Frankie Lymon! "*Why do birds sing so gay, and lover's await the break of day*". The break of day. When the darkness gives way to the light, Gene thought.

Group after group performed. Tony Williams, of the Platters. Danny Rapp, of Danny & The Juniors, who died by his own hand. Interesting that one of Danny's songs was called "Sometimes (When I'm All Alone")". How alone must Danny have been to have wanted to end his life?

Then the star came to the stage. It was The King. Elvis Presley! Gene thought he died and went to heaven. *Maybe I did.*

Elvis finished his set with one of the songs from his spiritual side—"How Great Thou Art". The happiness that Gene saw was on everyone's face. They all had a glow.

When it was time to get up, Gene continued to explore the Carousel. It was a spinning oasis. After some time, he came upon his parents, who had been gone for some twenty years. Heaven was all that he thought it would be.

People of faith, no matter what denomination, always look toward heaven as the place where they will be reunited with their departed loved ones. And there they were. They were as inseparable as they had been on earth. Beautiful. Gene screamed, joyfully, to get their attention. Strangely, they couldn't hear him. They looked in his direction, but didn't see him. They got up and walked away, arm in arm. Gene, left alone and confused, moved on.

He came upon people he knew when he was growing up. He came upon friends. There were his sports idols. All there. Gene was beside himself. He spoke to every one of them. They all looked past him, seemingly, without hearing him.

Everywhere that Gene went, he came upon the gray people. They looked confused, mostly. From head to toe, they were covered in the reminder of the disaster that they had experienced. Some still clutched handbags and laptops, as if they hadn't yet learned that they wouldn't need them anymore.

And the strangest thing. As if a mirror to the world they left, some of them clutched pictures to their chests. Gene imagined that this was some sort of connection. Maybe their live counterparts, the other half of their lives were, at this very instant, clutching their pictures, hoping that they were still alive. They were talking to each other and didn't know it.

Their challenges in life were now finished and so insignificant. Now they could rest and recharge. This was everlasting glory.

Behind the gray people, there stood Gene's son Chris. He was wearing his football jersey and he was staring right through Gene. In his amazement Gene was, for a moment, speechless. His tears washed his face . . . and he spoke. All he could say, before breaking up, was "Chris". Like his parents, Gene's son never responded. After the longest moment of both of their lives, Chris turned and walked away. In his back pocket was an open bottle of scotch.

Gene traveled for what seemed like days, or even months. He passed many buildings. There was the one that was his home, when he was a boy. It had long been gone, demolished by bulldozers and progress. Yet, there it was, whole and new and beautiful.

His 57 Chevy was parked in front of the building. That car met its demise at the hands of the junkyard crane operator thirty years ago. How could this be? Then, the strangest sight of all. Gene came upon the buildings known as The World Trade Center! They were as majestic as he remembered them to be. My God, they were intact!

This was a concept that Gene couldn't wrap his mind around. *Things go to heaven too!*

Not only does a soul spend eternal peace but, as if a security blanket to a child, the physicality of his life was also present. Familiar things bring a peace, a solace.

Strangely, or not, none of the terrorists, who took down the buildings and killed so many people were there to be found. Perhaps the Islam Heaven was in a different place. Maybe not.

Gene continued his quest. And all the while he noticed that he was being followed by a man holding a beautiful little girl. At the man's side, was a dopey looking dog. It was Butchie Sullivan. *Who was this guy*, Gene thought. He would never find out.

So he continued to look for his love. Now it was Gene and his entourage. Geri was there . . . somewhere. He searched and he searched some more. He couldn't find her. After a time, he came upon the Operator of the Carousel, a dark man of Middle Eastern decent.

*It was God.* How could he look like this, Gene mused. God looked like Jeffrey Hunter, the almost beautiful actor whom Gene had watched in the movies when he was a kid. The man playing God for the popcorn eating crowd.

Logic would dictate that, if the story of the Bible took place in the Middle East, then God the Father must be of Middle Eastern roots and looks. Gene never quite grasped that if there was Jesus Christ, the son of God, and then God himself, how is it that we pray to one God. God Almighty. Did God send himself to the earth? Nevertheless, there was God.

He was wearing beautiful white garments. His hair was pure white. And he operated the massive Carousel. Who else would have control over such a massive structure? "Please, your holiness, I'm looking for my wife, Geri. Can you help me?" The Almighty, the only one who heard Gene . . . acknowledged his presence, looked at him, kissed him on both cheeks and told him that she's not here on the carousel. He told him that she didn't make it. Gene was devastated. He had vowed to be with her for eternity.

WHEN A GLASS BREAKS

# FORTY THREE

" ***CLEAR!***"

That's all he heard. Then, "Good morning, Gene". Gene opened his eyes. He looked around and saw the stark hospital room. There were flowers on the window sill. There were cards. There was a Bible. Outside the window, it was snowing. Snowing? It was now late October and old man winter paid an early visit. This would mean that . . . .

"Yes", said the Doctor, as if he could read Gene's mind. You have been out for over a month. "A coma", he said. "But we all knew you would come back and here you are". Maybe, Gene thought, it was all a dream. The Carousel, his parents . . . . was it a dream? Or did he leave this world?

The Doctor told him that he had to be revived. His worse fears became a reality. They couldn't save Geri. Gene slipped into a depression that seemed even more harmful than the crash.

In a week or so, Gene made the transition to rational. It had been a very bumpy trip. The questions all resolved. Or were they? He still didn't know if he had a dream or if he had, in fact, visited the eternal light called Heaven. It was so vivid to him. Either way, he viewed it as a sign that Geri wasn't accepted into heaven. But why?

At that instant, he remembered the crash. He saw the little girl and the dog in the car.

*My God, Geri must have killed the little child and kept driving!* It was at that very instant that he felt the need to hold her and help her through this. There could be no life without Geri. Knowing that he had to be with her, it became clear that he must do whatever it took. He could no longer view Heaven as his eternal goal. He must kill so that he could face the fire and rejoin Geri.

# FORTY FOUR

OCTOBER 28TH—A NEW Jersey postal worker is diagnosed with inhalation Anthrax.

A World Trade Center Memorial Service, attended by victim's families, including the McGaffs, is held in New York City at Ground Zero, amidst the still smoldering ruins. The still smoldering ruins. Broken remnants of what were once happy lives were still smoldering . . . . suffocating.

It was early November when Gene finally got back to normalcy. That is, whatever normalcy there could be in this world without Geri. Part of his recovery process was alot of counseling sessions. He was late getting to the office for his first day back. He was nervous. Perhaps because he knew that he would face a lot of hugs and best wishes from his fellow inmates at Ruby's company. His biggest reception, not a surprise, was from Rosie. She had gone to the market and bought some hazelnut coffee, Gene's favorite. Usually she served only the grade B coffee that Ruby provided for the company. There he sat, at Rosie's Place . . . . with Rosie the Angel.

After some time, Gene went back downstairs to face his day. Years of abuse in his life made him callous and angry. Now the ultimate had happened to him. Geri was gone.

He went to his office. His routine was not the same. He didn't check messages. He didn't pull up the current sales report. He just sat for a moment. Then he got up and went straight to Ruby's office. He glided by the Executive Assistant's desk. She was beautiful. Normally, Gene would stop to talk with her.

He didn't knock, but instead walked right in to Ruby's office. He left the door opened behind him. Ruby was on the phone with the Orient, his bank. Gene walked to the corner of the lavish office. He grabbed the free standing mirror and walked it over to Ruby's desk. The mirror was normally positioned so that anyone sitting, in front of Ruby's desk, would always be distracted by their own image, while Ruby would drill them.

He rested the mirror directly in front of Ruby's desk. First startled, then shaking, then his eyes welled up, the way a coward's did when someone bigger stood up to him. Then Gene, in a low, almost whispering voice, started singing. Singing! Singing?

*"Ruby Ruby, I wa want you. Like a ghost I'm gonna haunt you".* A touch of Dion for Ruby baby.

He repeated the verse and then again. When Ruby had gathered the courage to scream for help, Gene pulled out his 45 caliber and politely whispered . . . . "Don't". There was silence for about ten seconds. The only explanation Gene offered was—"You're a bad guy, Ruby. And bad guys sometimes get what's coming". Ruby was a frequent visitor to the tanning salon and was always the picture of good health. Not anymore. He was as white as the walls.

*"Ruby Ruby, I wa want you. Like a ghost I'm gonna haunt you"*

"What do you want? I'll give you anything" said the slug. Ruby's quivering voice was not low. In a couple of minutes, the crowd began to gather outside the office. Yet, no one called the Police.

*"Each time I see you, Ruby, my heart cries. I tell you I'm gonna shoot you right between the eyes".*

"It's not me that you are going to pay, Ruby. I don't want your money. I want something else, but we'll get to that". We're gonna make some things right, Rube. But, we're gonna be smart about it. I know that you have a private account where you keep all the money that you stole from your Asian financial partners. The reason I know this? You just can't help opening that big mouth. That's where the money is going to come from. Share the wealth a bit. And nobody can know. Because if the Government finds out, all your money will be gone, whether or not you get out of this alive."

Ruby's tears came down and his right arm began to shake.

"You have millions in there, don't you, you sorry excuse for a human being. Get Norman in here. Pick up the phone, now, and get Norman in here." Ruby didn't need the phone. Norman was right outside the door. He entered the room slowly. He was as white as Ruby. "Hello Norman, nice of you to join us".

"Do what he wants, Norman" "What do you want? How much?"

"Oh, I don't want anything. Money doesn't mean much anymore. A million each to two accounts, Norman. I figure that, after taxes, these accounts will still be very fat.

Since you pay your employees by direct deposit, you already have the account information. All you have to do is call the slug at the bank, who knows all about that account. I wonder what his share is. But, I digress. Two people, Norman. Mrs. McGaff and Rosie. A million each. Do it now. It was a nice thing that you did, Ruby, having your very own bank offer your employees advantageous interest programs just for keeping their money there. You're a wonderful man, Ruby . . . . *Ruby Ruby, I wa want you. Like a ghost, I'm gonna haunt you.*

Gene stood patiently, pointing the gun. It took just a few phone calls from Ruby to the Bank President. There was some whispering, but Gene didn't care. Now, I want you to have the bank send proof of these transfers now. They can fax them right here to your fax number. "Do it. And, if you don't, your backers will find out in a hurry that the money exists. If you do, I'm going to let you keep the rest. Understood?" No response.

The next sound, exactly eight minutes later, was the fax machine. Two Proofs of Transfer, one after the other came over.

"Bring them to me", Gene said to Norman. "When he looked at them, he had two reactions.

One was to laugh. The money was withdrawn from the account of Ruby's 10 year old daughter. "Cute". His other reaction was to instruct Norman to fax them to the attention of Mr. J. R. Meehan, President of Gene's bank, and personal friend. Norman complied.

Gene picked up the phone, never moving his gun from Ruby's direction. "J. R., how are you. On your fax machine are the two documents. I told you this guy was crooked. I just need you to verify that these transfers are legit. I'll wait." In just a few minutes, Gene heard what he wanted to hear, thanked J.R. and listened for a moment. Said goodbye.

"Thanks Ruby. Thanks Norman." The rest is all yours. And Gene began to sing.

*"Norman. Norman My Love"* "Remember Sue Thompson, Rube? Cute little blond who could sing with a smile in her voice." Geri used to tell Gene that he had a steel trap for a mind. How does he remember all these songs?

# FORTY FIVE

"OK, GUYS, YOU'RE almost there", Gene's voice, coldly echoing from Ruby's marble desk." Gene raised the gun. "ShBoom". At the word Boom, Gene jolted the gun upward as if it went off. He continued singing. On the second Boom, he pointed at Norman. On the third, he pointed at himself. The fourth Boom belonged to Ruby Baby.

Now he was on a roll, singing at the top of his lungs. "ShBoom ShBoom, yada da da dad a dad dad a, Sh Boom." He sang some more. It was like musical chairs. Who would be left without a chair. Who would get the Boom? It took what seemed to be an hour. But it was seconds. Who needs a chair? Who doesn't have a chair? Who doesn't have a chair! The gun went off. Was it the ceiling? Norman? Not a likely candidate. But why not? He was Ruby's executioner. Was it Ruby?

One of them said good bye.

# FORTY SIX

THE CHURCH WAS quiet. There was no Mass going on. The statues stood, so lifelike. Each station of the cross told the story of Jesus Christ to the empty pews. The confessional boxes were empty. It was an interesting paradox, Gene always thought. You go to the Lord's house, but you don't tell the Lord your sins. You sit in the box and you tell another man.

To the right of the Confessionals were the candles. The flames were reaching up, as if to God, to get his attention. There were 20 candles per row, all uniform, like a purposeful army.

From left to right, the first row flames were looking to the "sky". They were all burning.

# FORTY SEVEN

THE HOUSE WAS quiet. Like the sound of one hand clapping. The living room was unchanged. It was still resplendent, in all its beauty. All the animal statues—the two rocking horses and the metal giraffe,were standing guard.

December now. Christmastime. The Christian world was celebrating the birth . . . . the hope of new beginnings.

Down the hall, the pictures were mostly straight. Pictures are inanimate. Yet they have their own ideas on how they should hang. So, like a calculating little child, they wait for their opportunity to shift. To be askew. Like the lives they depicted.

In a ten foot stretch of wall, one can see an entire life span of a loved one. Geri's dad followed a journey that took 84 years to complete. Yet, three and a half steps now covered the time. When a glass breaks, it is transformed into thousands of separate "stories". A short pilgrimage down the hall and the glass is miraculously back together.

The television was on, the morning show anchor was telling whoever Neilson was counting that it was going to be a great day. Gene sat up in bed, sipped his coffee, and absorbed the talking head's dialog between his ears. The morning was always a time for reflection. It was a natural compliment to the night time prayers.

In the doorway, a shadow . . . . The familiar and beautiful sound.

"More coffee sweetheart?"